LIGHT RAIL REVIEW

GW00722737

CONTENTS

Published by Platform 5 Publishing Ltd., and the Light Rail Transit Association.

© Light Rail Transit Association, Albany House, Petty France, London SW1H 9EA and Platform 5 Publishing Ltd., Wyvern House, Old Forge Business Park, Sark Road, Sheffield S2 4HG, England.

ISBN 1 872524 44 3

Printed in England by BDC Printing Services Ltd., Slack Lane, Derby.

Further copies of this publication may be obtained from Platform 5 Publishing Ltd. or the Light Rail Transit Association at the above addresses, price £7.50. Please add 10% (UK) 20% (overseas) to cover postage and packing.

Construction work on the triangle or 'delta junction' in Sheffield. to the left of the picture is the new Pond's Forge swimming complex and in the centre the AMEC-designed bowstring-arch bridge which will take the Supertrams into Commercial Street and then through Central Sheffield to Middlewood. The bridge in the foreground leads to the Interchange station behind the Midland railway station and on to the Mosborough route
Peter Fox

FUNDING FIASCO

Midland Metro Told to Wait

by Bob Tarr, Director-General, West Midlands PTE

8th June 1992 was a day that Centro would prefer to forget. It was the day that Secretary of State for Transport John MacGregor informed the Chairman of the Passenger Transport Authority that we would not be able to start work on the construction of Line 1 of Midland Metro in 1993.

It had been increasingly apparent that the warning bells for public expenditure were beginning to be rung by the government following the General Election in April. However, we understood from the Department of Transport that, based upon its extremely good appraisal, Line 1 was backed by the Department and would be put forward to the Treasury with the Department's backing for funding starting in 1993/94.

In Autumn 1991, Roger Freeman, Minister of State responsible for public transport had agreed that Centro should spend £1.5 million on further development of the Line 1 proposal, particularly the obtaining of a firm price for construction of Line 1 – Mr Freeman agreed to pay £0.75 million in grant to Centro to help meet these costs. The absence of a firm price had been described by Mr Freeman as the one missing component in the appraisal. To obtain a firm price it was, of course, necessary to go out to tender and Centro did so, starting with prequalification under the European Community rules in late 1991.

Line 1 is to be built through a design. build, operate and maintain concession (a DBOM). This method had been chosen not, by any means because we in Centro preferred it over the alternatives, including the traditional approaches, but because it was favoured by Government. Government believes that the DBOM approach ensures the maximum involvement of the private sector and the maximum contribution towards the cost of such projects by the private sector and transfers all or a large part of the risk from the public sector to the private sector.

By June of this year Centro had selected 3 consortia who were poised to begin the detailed tendering process. They had received all the tendering documents and were due, the day after Mr MacGregor's announcement, to pay their tendering bonds (a deposit to guarantee they would in due course actually complete the tendering process). All 3 tenderers DID pay their deposits, but, unfortunately, in the light of Mr MacGregor's announcement we had to return those deposits and suspend the tendering process because, obviously, the ground rules as to when the project will take place had been changed by his announcement.

We were surprised to learn from Mr Freeman that the Secretary of State thought he was being helpful in telling us the bad news as soon as possible. In fact, because it necessarily caused the suspension of the tendering process (and indeed no tenderer would tender in such circumstances) it was not possible to satisfy Mr Freeman's declared wish to get a firm price. In addition, we had an extra hurdle to jump in that when the tendering process was to restart, the tenderers would need more than a little assurance that their time and effort and money would not be wasted (it is reckoned that a DBOM tenderer is likely to spend between £0.2 million and £0.5 million in preparing his tender). Tenderers are prepared to take the ordinary risks of winning or losing the tender competition but do want to be reasonably sure that someone will get the contract and the project will go ahead.

However, we did decide to restart the tendering process, following the Government's announcement of a "going for growth" strategy in November. Four private consortia have been invited to submit their tenders by the end of February 1992. The consortia are as follows:

BALFOUR-BEATTY – SIEMENS JOINT VENTURE (Balfour Beatty Ltd. and Siemens plc).

CENTRAM (Taylor-Woodrow Construction Holdings Ltd and Ansaldo Trasporti SpA).

JOHN MOWLEM – GEC ALSTHOM JOINT VENTURE (John Mowlem & Co. plc and GEC Alsthom).

EUROTRANSIT (Norwest Holst Holdings Ltd., Tilbury Douglas Construction Ltd. and AEG – Westinghouse Transport Systems GmbH.

Midland Metro Line 1 has been through the most rigorous appraisal of any light rail scheme so far – and pretty certainly more rigorous than any previous provincial public transport scheme and, probably, highway scheme. It is the first scheme to be subjected to the full rigour of Circular 3/89 It has survived that appraisal comfortably with the combination of user benefits as represented by fares and non-user benefits related to transport (such as decongestion, roads investment avoided and accident costs savings) considerably exceeding the costs. And that's without counting any of the non-transport or "softer"non-user benefits, such as economic regeneration and employment, environmental benefits etc.

The deferring of Midland Metro Line 1 seems to be a straight case of the right project having the wrong timing, in that it has come up for government support at just the time that Government is putting everything (or nearly everything) on hold.

So where do we go now? Well we are certainly not retreating back into our shells to sulk or feel sorry for ourselves and the West Midlands (though we do!).

The things we HAVE achieved in 1992 is to get the Royal Assent for our Lines 2 and 3 of Midland Metro and we still have before Parliament 2 Bills which are both unopposed and should be into law by around March 1993. Taken together, all our Parliamentary Powers will then enable us to build the foundations of the West Midlands light rail network – some 80 km of routes, the biggest network so far empowered by Parliament. Our ultimate aspiration, as is well known, is for some 200 km of routes, but this time is, of course, long term.

We are undertaking advance works costing some £3 million on the part of the Metro which will share formation with the proposed heavy rail link from Moor St/Snow Hill to Smethwick West. Doing this now, before either scheme starts, was already proposed and the Government have given credit for it – by preparing the formation in advance we will save some £3.5 million on the total cost of the 2 schemes if they were done quite separately. These advance works should be finished by March 1993.

To say we are champing at the bit to get on and build Midland Metro is to seriously understate our enthusiasm. We are now working, with our consultants, on the detailed appraisal/justification for Lines 2 and 3. We will obviously, in the light of the delay in starting construction of Line 1, look to see whether we should be bolder in terms of what should be included in Phase 1 of construction – we couldn't before because we did not have the powers through Parliament, we now do have. We look to the example of Sheffield which is undertaking a first phase costing some £230 million compared with the expected £100 million of Line 1 of Midland Metro.

There is, of course, some benefit in not being the first. We believed we have, through the generous co-operation of our colleagues in Greater Manchester and South Yorkshire PTEs, been able to build upon their experience with their own LRT schemes. In particular we have put a lot of effort into ensuring that the DBOM system will actually deliver to the West Midlands what the West Midland wants and needs. An area into which we have put enormous effort is the whole question of aesthetics and visual appearance and environmental intrusion — even to the extent of employing public artists to help write the design standards and guidance — so as to get the same sort of quality of design that has been so magnificently achieved in Birmingham in Centenary Square and the International Convention Centre.

Mr Freeman has told the Members if the West Midlands Passenger Transport Authority how disappointed he is himself that he will not have the resources to allow the project to proceed in 1993/94 and that he hopes the economy will improve so that he is able to get some additional resources as soon as possible, though there is no prospect for 1993/4. He is undoubtedly sincere in this. He has explained that he only has £50 million per annum for light rail schemes and that, in effort, Sheffield has first call on that (because it is a scheme already in progress) for, effectively, the next 3 years or so. He has said that Midland Metro Line 1 is the number 1 scheme on a list of one. There is no competition at the moment because no-one else is so far advance in obtaining powers and develop-

ing their schemes. We are, naturally, aware and apprehensive that if we have to wait 3 or 4 years we may no longer be on a list of one. We will still be pretty sure that Midland Metro will fully justify the number 1 spot however long the list is!

There is, finally, an irony that at the very time Mr MacGregor was informing us that he would not be able to allow a start next year, the 7 Metropolitan Councils of the West Midlands (+ the PTA) were finalising what is called the "Balanced Package" of transport schemes of all sorts, roads and public transport, which are proposed for 1993/94. The unanimous view of all 8 authorities is that the number 1 priority in the West Midlands is Midland Metro Line 1. It is only the customs and practices of the Department of Transport which prevents resources being allocated according to an overall view of priorities and instead compartmentalises programmes as roads (most of the total in England & Wales outside London and the South-East) and public transport (a tiny programme by comparison with roads). Taken together with the very uneven playing field on which appraisal of roads v public transport schemes are conducted one feels there is an attitude or culture change of sizeable proportions needed within the Department of Transport quite apart from the hopefully fairly short term problems with the economy and thus for transport investment. There are some hopeful signs that the Department is at least willing to consider seriously the "Balanced Package approach".

Bob Tarr

Bob Tarr is the Director-General of the West Midlands Passenger Transport Executive.

LIGHT RAIL REVIEW

FRENCH PIONEER

Nantes – France's First Modern LRT System

by Peter Fox

THE NANTES CONURBATION

Nantes is the largest city of the French province of Bretagne (Britanny). The Nantes connurbation consists of 20 different towns. It is the most important of its kind in the west of France and is located at the estuary of the river Loire about 50 km from the Atlantic Coast. It is the seventh largest connurbation in France (after Paris, Lyon, Marseille, Lille, Bordeaux and Toulouse), and covers 473 square kilometres. The population in 1991 was just under 500,000.

A syndicate was formed in 1982 so that central services could be provided for the ½ million residents of this connurbation. This was known as SIMAN (Syndicat Intercommunal à Vocation Multiple de l' Agglomération Nantaise), but since 1st January 1992 has been known as the 'District de l' Agglomération Nantaise', or 'the District' for short.

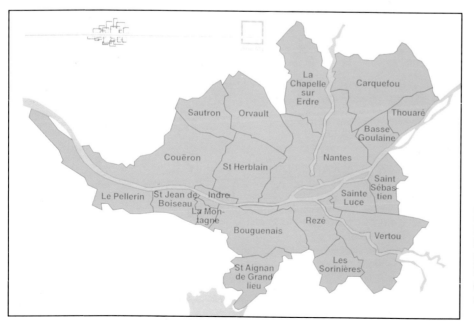

◀ The Nantes connurbation, now known as 'the District'.
Agglomération Nantaise

▶ The station at Gare SNCF (the railway station) is quite attractive with trees planted along the platforms. The platform furniture (shelters, seats, ticket machines, maps etc) has been standardised for almost all stations. A clean, uncluttered look is apparent.
Peter Fox

▲ On leaving Bellevue, line 1 runs along the centre of the Boulevard Romanet on ballasted railway track, attractively lined with bushes and pampas grass clumps. Car 325, with a low-floor centre section, is seen approaching Jamet.
Peter Fox

◀ The western terminus of Nantes line 1 at Bellevue, showing tram No. 303 as delivered as a two-section car. This photograph illustrates the provision of car-parking and bus connections. To the right is a suburban shopping centre.
Peter Fox

▶ Médiathèque, central Nantes, with car 312, still in its two-section guise.
Peter Fox

HISTORICAL BACKGROUND

Nantes had the first horse-drawn omnibus network in the world in 1825, and in 1879 was the first French city to instal a compressed air driven tramway. By 1911, Nantes was completely served by trams with 39 route-km and 12 million passengers per annum. One of the compressed-air-powered trams has been preserved (see opposite). Electrification took place between 1913 and 1917 and by 1932 there were 20 routes centered on the Place du Commerce. This tramway system, which was run by a private company with no subsidy, was finally closed in 1958. This left a very poor public transport service in Nantes, operated by an ageing bus fleet.

One idea put forward by the municipality in 1971 was to run a regular service of diesel railcars on SNCF lines radiating from Nantes. Called the *metro nantais*, it was rejected because of its high costs and poor accessibility.

The concession of the private company, CNTC, ended in 1975, and on 1st January 1976, the arrangements detailed below came into operation.

ORGANISATION OF PUBLIC TRANSPORT

Public transport is operated by SEMITAN (Société d' Economie Mixte des Transports en commun de l' Agglomération Nantaise). This is a semi-public company owned as follows:
- The District (65%)
- Nantes Chamber of Commerce & Industry (10%)
- The Local Savings Bank (Caisse d' Epargne et de Prévoyance de Nantes) (10%)
- TRANSCET S.A. (14.95%)
- Three user groups (0.05%)

SEMITAN runs the network, but the budget is set by the District. The abbreviation 'TAN' is used for marketing purposes.

THE NEW TRAMWAY

The oil crisis of the 70s led to the French government taking the initiative of recommending medium-sized cities to investigate the possibility of reintroducing tramways. The state would pay 50% of the infrastructure cost. Nantes decided to take the lead in this, the result being line one which opened between Haluchère and Commerce on 7th January 1985 and between Bellevue and Commerce on 18th February 1985. The rest of the cost of this line was met by the *versement transport*, a local payroll tax which can be levied by connurbations with a population greater than 300,000. Companies with ten or more employees have to pay this tax, which in Nantes was set at 1.5%.

This first line runs from Bellevue to the west of Nantes via the city centre and railway station to Haluchère in north east Nantes. It is of interest to note that between Gare Maritime through the Place du Commerce to a point between Moutonnerie and Hôpital Bellier, the route followed one of the original tramway routes. From then on to Haluchère, the route uses a portion of SNCF Chateaubriant freight line. This line had a formation wide enough to take two tracks of mainline railway, but only one track was ever put down. It has proved possible to build a double track LRT route at the side of the SNCF single track.

At both Bellevue and Haluchère there are interchanges with buses, the bus services being integrated with the LRT system. A new depot and head office for SEMITAN was constructed at Dalby, just past before Hôpital Bellier. As well as being a maintenance centre for the LRT system, there is also a bus garage, the video surveillance system and PA system for stations as well as the control system for the electric supply. An extension of the line from Haluchère to La Beaujoire was opened on 22nd April 1989 making the total length of the line 12.6 km with 24 stations. There is also a bus-tram interchange at this new terminus.

CHARACTERISTICS OF THE SYSTEM

The Nantes Light Rail System, being the first new system in France, was necessarily a pioneer. The vehicles themselves were originally intended to be a new French standard tram. However, no provision was made for disabled passengers in these two-section cars and when the Grenoble system opened, it was with a new design of tram with low-floor entrances to enable mobility-impaired people to have access. The Grenoble design has certainly at the present time, become a French standard, although a completely different design of car is being built for the new light rail system at present being constructed in Strasbourg.

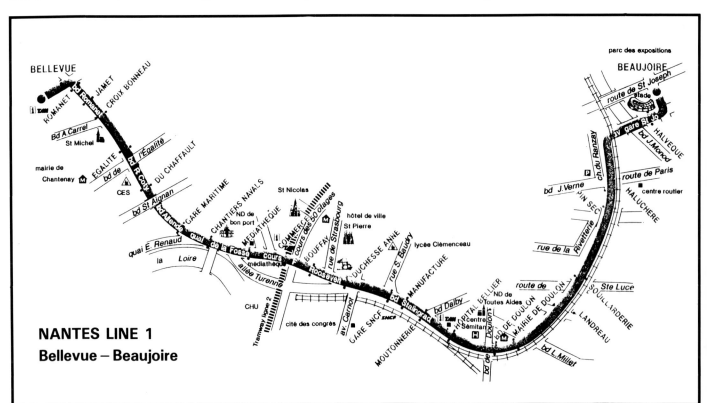

NANTES LINE 1
Bellevue – Beaujoire

Inside the new depot at Trocardière (at the south end of line 2) on 26th September 1992, with museum piece 18 (a Mékarski compressed air driven tram of 1878) alongside Alsthom articulated tram 314 of 1984 with a newly-installed centre section.
M.R. Taplin

The track for the system is of two types. Where the route runs alongside the road, tramway rail is used with paving between the rails. Where the line is completely segregated from the road, for example between Dalby and the terminus at La Beaujoire, railway-type track is used with sleepers and railway rail. The method of construction of the tramway sections is quite simple. The tramway rails are layed on sleepers consisting of concrete blocks with metal ties. These are then filled in with aggregate before laying the paving slabs or block pavers. Sound deadening is provided by blocks of rubber which are placed on the sides of the rails.

Platforms are low (200 mm above rail level) and it is necessary for passengers to step up into the vehicles. The problem of access for mobility-impaired people has been solved by the building of new low-floor centre sections, which have been fitted retrospectively to all cars. This has also obviated the need to use coupled pairs of cars for capacity purposes. The stations themselves are generally of a standard design and contain ticket machines, passenger information displays and waiting shelters.

The trams run on sight over the whole line, except that there are block signals on the segregated section between Dalby and Haluchère (see below). There are three road crossings on private rights-of-way alongside the SNCF track controlled by lights. Speed restrictions are 70 km/h between Dalby and the end of the segregated track near La Beaujoire, 40 km/h between Médiathèque and Gare SNCF and 60 km/h elsewhere.

LINE ONE IN DETAIL

Line one starts at Bellevue to the west of Nantes. Here there is an interchange with buses plus car parking as well as a shopping centre. The route follows a mainly segregated alignment in the centre of a dual carriageway. This area is a residential area. At Du Chaffault, the line runs on railway track on quite a steep gradient under a main road bridge. The line carries on to Gare Maritime and then becomes a tramway running at the side of the main road. This is a mainly industrial area. The line then runs past the dockyard and passes the Médiathèque (the library). The line is now running through the centre of Nantes and after the Place du Commerce, the Chateau des Ducs de Bretagne is passed on the left, just before the railway station on the right. The line continues at the side of the road and crosses over to join the segregated alignment alongside the SNCF freight line between Moutonnerie and Dalby, passing the depot on the left. The route is now heading for a mainly residential area. At no point on the whole route is the route shared with general road traffic, although there are a number of street crossings. Just after Haluchère the LRT route has to cross the SNCF freight line on the level. However, since the LRT route runs to the west of the SNCF line at this point, but requires to diverge to the east, there is a *chicane* in the track where the SNCF freight line is crossed. This crossing is controlled by SNCF signalling. Eventualy the line reaches the terminus at La Beaujoire.

▲ The original north-eastern terminus of line 1 was at Haluchère where three-section car No. 327 is seen arriving. Feeder buses arrive at the adjacent purpose-built bus station.   *Peter Fox*

◄ The extension of line 1 to Beaujoire necessitated a crossing of the SNCF freight line. Car 330 is seen approaching Haluchère negotiating the chicane in the LRT track across the SNCF line.
Peter Fox

▼ The pleasantly-wooded Beaujoire terminus.   *Peter Fox*

▲ Dalby depot on 10th September 1992. As well as a number of three-section cars, two centre sections can be seen awaiting fitting to earlier 2-section cars. *Peter Fox*

▶ Approaching the southern terminus of line 2, car 319, still running as a two-section car, proceeds along Avenue d'Anjou, Rezé. This street has been traffic-calmed and is now a tramway with road vehicles only permitted for access purposes. *Peter Fox*

▼ One of two non-standard stations on line 2, Pont Rousseau has been designed to fit in with an existing avenue of trees. *Peter Fox*

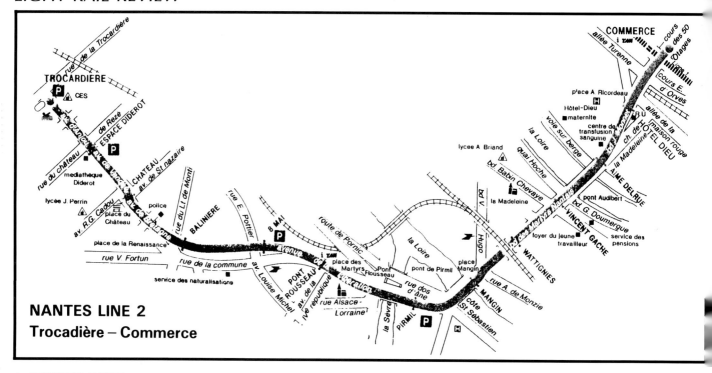

NANTES LINE 2
Trocadière – Commerce

A SECOND LINE

The success of line one in attracting passengers (45,000 per day by mid 1986, 38% being former car drivers or passengers) prompted SIMAN to study a second line from the town of Rezé (to the south of the Loire) to Nantes centre. The decision to build this was taken in 1988. On 12th January 1990 SIMAN considered an extension of this line north to the town of Orvault, serving the University en route, and on 29th June of that year the board voted unanimously to proceed with this. Meanwhile, patronage of line 1 was growing and in 1991 an average of 65,000 passengers per day was carried.

Line 2 should have opened from Trocadierè to 50 Otages on 7th September 1992, but only actually opened as far as Commerce on that date, as the line to 50 Otages was not finished until December. Commerce station was also only partially finished by 10th September, even though services were operating. An official opening procession from Trocadière to Commerce took place on 26th September, headed by trams 308 and 324 with green bow ribbons!

By September 1993 the Cours des 50 Otages, previously a double four-lane dual carriageway, will be replaced by the tramway, a two-lane highway and a two-lane busway separated by rows of trees, with large pedestrian areas. This is seen as a major environmental improvement.

LINE TWO (PHASE 1) IN DETAIL

Leaving Commerce station, there is a 90° crossing with line 1. There is a double-track junction with line 1 from north to east, plus a single track one from east to south. The line runs in the centre reservation of dual carriageway roads almost all the way to Trocadierè, with tram rails generally being used with paving between them. Between the first station at Hôtel Dieu and the second one at Aime Delrue is a three track section which will be used for reversing future short workings between University and the City Centre. The River Loire is crossed twice with the Ile Sainte-Anne, in between. At Pirmil there is a bus—LRT interchange and also a park and ride facility. No fewer than 10 bus routes feed the tramway here. Pont Rousseau station, the first one in the town of Rezé, is completely different from all other stations, having been given special environmental treatment to blend in with an avenue of trees. The next station is 8 Mai, where there is also a park and ride facility. From here to Ballinière the line runs on ballasted track with railway rail. Approaching the Rezé

terminus at Trocadière the route runs down the traffic-calmed Avenue d' Anjou, which has become tram and access only. There is a headshunt at Trocadière which then leads to a new servicing depot with holding sidings.

THE VEHICLES

As built the vehicles were of two-section design with power bogies at each end and a trailer bogie in the centre. Overall length was 28.50 m, but this has been increased to 39.15 m with the addition of the new low-floor centre secion. Doors are of the swing plug type. Each power bogie has a 275 kW d.c. monomoter fully suspended in the centre of the frame. Transmission is by cardan shafts with two-stage reduction gear boxes. Wheels are of the S.A.B. resilient type. Regenerative and rheostatic braking is provided, together with electrically-activated disc brakes and magnetic track brakes for emergency use. Seating capacity has been increased from 60 to 72 with the addition of the low-floor centre-section, and standing capacity has been increased from 108 to 162 (4/m^2) or from 178 to 269 under crush conditions (6.6/m^2)

FUTURE PLANS

Construction of the next phase of line 2 to the University is due to be completed by September 1993 and the rest of the line to Orvault by September 1994. The total length of line 2 will then be 14 km, with 6 stations in Rezé, 23 in Nantes and 2 in Orvault.

Line 3 will run from St. Herblain in the north-east of the connurbation to St. Sebastien-Vertou in the south-west. The exact route is yet to be decided, but a junction for the line to the north-west has already been laid, in Cours de 50 Otages.

TICKETS

Tickets are issued from automatic machines, fares being as follows:

Single Journey	7FF
Carnet of 5 tickets	25FF
Carnet of 10 tickets	45FF
day ticket	16FF
Weekly ticket	50FF

There is also a carnet of 10 tickets for persons entitled to reduced fares at 25FF.

Under consideration for the future is a combined park and ride ticket.

ERVICE FREQUENCY

he daytime frequency on line 1 is one am every 7 minutes Monday – Saturday, ith a 5 minute service in the Monday – Friday peak periods. On Sundays there is one tram every 20 minutes n the morning, with a 15 minute frequency in the afternoon. In the evening, frequencies wind down until after approx 1.30 there is only a 30 minute service. ervices generally run from around 05.00 06.30 on Sundays) to midnight.

The situation on line 2 is similar, except that the normal weekday service is one tram every 8 minutes, with a 6 minute eak frequency.

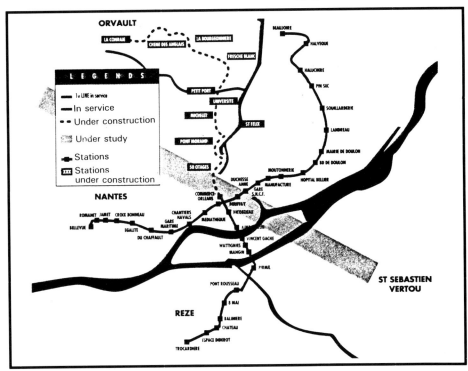

In Cours des 50 Otages at its junction with Rue de Feltre the pointwork has been installed for a possible line 3 to Sillon de Bretagne in the north-west suburbs. n the background can be seen trams decorated for the 26th September 1992 opening ceremony (see page 12).
M.R. Taplin

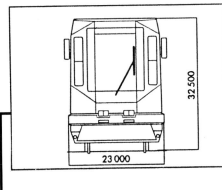

NANTES TRAM WITH LOW-FLOOR CENTRE SECTION

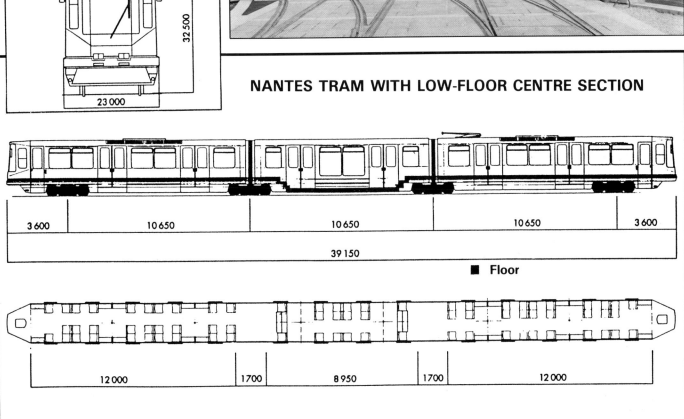

■ **Floor**

The other station with a non-standard design is Pirmil, a purpose built bus-tram interchange with a park and ride facility.
Peter Fox

▲◄ The new ticket machines on line 2 are simple and convenient.
Peter Fox

▲ Tracklaying in progress on Cours des 50 Otages.
Peter Fox

◄ After the opening ceremony the decorated trams entered public service on line 2. 331 and 332 are on the three-track section south of Hotel Dieu that will form a reversing facility for University – Centre short workings from 1994.
M.R. Taplin

THE GUIDED BUS
A Credible Alternative to Light Rail?

by Ian Yearsley, Michael Taplin and Peter Fox

HISTORY

The guided bus is an idea that will not go away. The German Ministry for Research and Technology (BMFT) assisted the two largest German bus manufacturers, Daimler Benz and MAN, to create projects in the late 1970s, with an extensive O-Bahn test track for Daimler Benz at Rastatt and another for MAN's electronic guidance system at its München factory. The MAN project never achieved commercial reliability, but the first installation of the O-Bahn for public use was at Essen in September 1980, where a 1.3-km reserved track section of the former tram route in Fulerumerstrasse was laid out with a concrete guideway for kerb-guided buses.

But guided buses have a much longer history than this. The idea of a bus running on a guideway is almost as old as that of the tramcar running on rails. William Joseph Curtis patented a horse bus with moveable flanges in 1856, and for nine months in 1859 it ran on the tracks of the Mersey Docks and Harbour Board. Little use seems to have been made of its road running facility except for journeys to and from the depot. In Salford John Greenwood laid down a line in 1861 based on the ''perambulating principle'' patented by John Haworth. The bus wheels ran on flat plates set flush with the road surface, and a centre-grooved plateway provided guidance through a retractable guide wheel which controlled the steering movement of the rotating fore-carriage of the bus.

On this system, which lasted until 1872, there was but a single track, and cars passing one another had to disengage

▲ The Volkshochschule stop in Essen is served by two tram routes and two bus routes that use the O-Bahn. Note how the metre-gauge tram tracks fit between the bus guideway.
M.R. Taplin

▼ A stop on the Essen guided busway in the centre of an urban motorway. Both diesel buses and duo-buses use this route. *Peter Fox*

and use the ordinary road for short distances. The system was claimed to be less troublesome to other traffic than George Train's step rail, used at Birkenhead in 1860 and London in 1861, also in the Potteries and Darlington. If Haworth's system had been generally adopted for horse tramways, the electric tramcar might well have emerged as a version of the present day GLT system, with flangeless, probably solid rubber-tyred, road wheels and a central guide mechanism, and the ability to run off the end of the guideway as a steered vehicle using one or other of the various systems of trackless trolleybus then being promoted. The present distinction between tram, trolleybus and bus would have been blurred.

Several features of Haworth's system, particularly the ability to run as a steered vehicle off the guideway, and to use a single track in both directions, are part of the present debate about guided buses. In Great Britain, now as then, close collaboration between the local authority and the operator is needed for the guided bus to succeed (the Salford local authority finally removed Greenwood's guideway, and sent him the bill for so doing).

One key difference between then and now is the reason for using guideways. Road surfaces, whether waterbound macadam, cobbles or stone sets, all offered a greater resistance to vehicle movement than did the smooth surfaces of rails or plateways. With the limited power of horse traction, smooth guideways could offer real productivity gains in terms of speed, people carried, and the working life of horses.

THE KERB-GUIDED BUS OR 'O-BAHN'

Today, however, the problem for the bus operator is not rough roads but congestion. Segregated public transport is an answer, but the cost of going underground or on viaduct is high. Segregated surface light rail is cheaper but the vehicles cost a lot more than mass-produced buses. It is not suprising that planners and bus manufacturers have cast around for ways of getting the bus to behave like a tram. The generous Federal research funds in Germany provided the catalyst for the development of the O-Bahn.

To operate on the O-Bahn, standard diesel buses are fitted with horizontal guide wheels ahead of the front axle, controlling the conventional Ackermann steering linkages. These guide wheels bear against 180-mm high vertical concrete kerbs, set 2.6 m apart. Tapering gauge sections with steel guides provide a lead-in to each section of guideway: short gaps for pedestrian crossings can be provided without guides. On the guideway the bus driver does not have to touch the steering wheel: the vehicles are steered manually on other sections of route.

Further guideway sections were opened in Essen in 1983, 1985 and 1988 to demonstrate O-Bahn sharing reserved track and tunnel operation with metre-gauge tramways, and also diesel/trolleybus duobus operation. Meanwhile in Adelaide plans for a light rail line to the north-east suburbs were cancelled abruptly with a change of government, as the incoming administration harked back to the German roots of much of the population in the area, and initiated discussions with Daimler Benz for the provision of an O-Bahn on the same alignment. The Adelaide busway was brought in to use in 1986, and extended in 1989.

The Tracline project in Birmingham, England, opened in 1984 using similar technology, but with double-deck vehicles. This became a victim of bus deregulation in 1986 because not all buses serving the route were equipped to use the guideway, and also because the guideway was on the least congested part of the route and offered little advantage therefore. The reservation was originally built for trams in 1926, not to bypass congestion, but because sleeper track construction was cheaper than street track and allowed the cars to run at greater speed. North American experience led Liverpool city engineer John Brodie to champion this form of construction from 1910 onwards, and others followed him.

Guided bus demonstration tracks and vehicles, using equipment from the dismantled Tracline project, have been created in operators' garage premises in Leeds and Rotherham, and there have been a number of proposals for systems in other British cities, including Cambridge, Hull, Luton and Newcastle-upon-Tyne. The Leeds project for sections of the A61 and A64 will go ahead in 1993/94 if government grant is forthcoming.

Essen, Germany

Essen is a major city in the Ruhrgebiet, the polycentric conurbation that embraces the major industrial area of western Germany from Krefeld to Dortmund. The city population is 620 000, but it is more important than the surrounding towns in terms of industry, employment and shopping. Essener Verkehrs AG operates a metre-gauge tram system that has through links to adjoining systems in Muelheim/Ruhr and Bochum-Gelsenkirchen. Since the 1970s this has been supplemented (and to a degree supplanted) by the standard-gauge Ruhr Stadtbahn, a new segregated light rail system. German railways (DB) provide local S-Bahn services through the conurbation, which thus has an excellent public transport network, all provided under the standard tarif system of the Verkehrsverbund Rhein-Ruhr.

When Federal research money was on offer for a guided bus demonstration project, EVAG offered the alignment of the partly single-track route 12, linking the city centre with Faengershof via Humboldstrasse. The side reservation alongside the city's West Cemetery was not wide enough to take two-way non-guided buses, so instead of the plan to create a dual-carriageway road served by buses (which was opposed by residents), the Federal money was used to create 1.2 km of busway for route 166, served by 21 Mercedes-Benz 0305G articulated buses and three 0305 rigid buses equipped with guide wheels. Public service started on 28th September 1980.

Phase two of the project was inaugurated in September 1983 when 1 km of metre-gauge tramway in Wittenbergstrasse was modified to demonstrate joint running of tramway and O-Bahn, the concrete beams (wooden beams were also trialled) for the bus tyres running just outside the tram rails. Trolleybus wiring was strung alongside the tram wire and automatic poling and depoling devices installed at each end of the demonstration section so that two prototype duobuses could be used. A fearsome joint tramway and O-Bahn point switch was installed using steel and hydraulics, but the lack of any subsequent comment in the German technical press leads one to believe that this was unsuccessful - certainly O-Bahn pointwork has never been mentioned since.

In January 1985 the city council decided to proceed with the third phase of the project, the conversion of the metre-gauge tramway in the median strip of the Ruhr motorway between Wasserturm and the suburb of Kray (4 km) to a dedicated O-Bahn, which could be through-routed into the city centre tram subways to give experience of a complete route run with duobuses and including tunnel operation under common signal control with trams and light rail trains. The decision to convert the high-quality Kray tramway was not popular with passengers, if only because shortly after the decision was taken a severe winter showed that fresh snowfall compacted under the tyres of O-Bahn buses produced ice which caused the service to be suspended until it could be broken up and swept away by hand. This meant that the access ramps to the motorway median had to have heated guideway surfaces.

18 Daimler-Benz 0405GTD articulated duobuses were ordered at a cost of DEM 800 000 each, of which EVAG had to find only 25 per cent, the balance being met by the Ministry of Research and Technology. Public service started in June 1986, with trolleybus wiring erected around the street loop in Kray and from Wasserturm in to the city centre subway, while electric operation along the motorway median was pro-

nised "later". Not suprisingly the integration of O-Bahn into the rail subway took longer to sort out, and was not inaugurated until September 1988. The whole third stage cost
DEM 68 million (with 75 per cent subsidy), while Daimler-
Benz is estimated to have spent DEM 100 million on O-Bahn
development, of which DEM 61 million came from the
Ministry.

In May 1989 the City Council adopted its Stadtbahn programme for the period to the year 2008, predicting a network
of six standard-gauge lines and five tram routes by then, and
making it clear that no further O-Bahn conversions were planned. Towards the end of 1990 work started to rebuild the
duobuses with offside doors, because the subway extension
from Porscheplatz to Altendorfer Strasse, due to open in 1991,
featured central platforms, which would be served by trams
and O-Bahn vehicles. Around this time the buses received
a new colour scheme for the City-Express marketing concept
for limited-stop services in the Rhein-Ruhr area. Routes 145
and 147 became CE45 and CE47.

The subway extension was inaugurated on 9th November
1991, after a month of trials to test out the systems, particularly
signalling and train control, with the increased frequency of

trams and buses passing through. This 1.5 km subway cost
DEM 184 million, of which the city of Essen contributed DEM
20 million. However, after only six days the O-Bahn services
had to be withdrawn from the subway and rerouted through
surface streets, because under operational conditions the com-
puterised train control system proved incapable of handling
the mixture of trams and buses at the necessary frequency.
Hopes that the problem could be resolved in May 1992 were
optimistic, but in the end the programmers had to admit defeat.
The only way the buses could return to the subway was to
reduce the frequency of one of the tram routes by running
coupled pairs of trams (to maintain passenger capacity), thus
freeing paths for the O-Bahn — a fine example of tramway
flexibility not possible with the guided bus operation. This
was scheduled for May 1993, when the CE45 and CE47 should
again be running underground in the city centre.

This appears to draw the line under O-Bahn development
in Germany, Daimler Benz's hopes that the city where its buses
are built, Mannheim, would opt for O-Bahn on a major new
fixed track line were dashed by the decision to build a
segregated tramway. However, perhaps to save face, a short
section of O-Bahn has been built in Mannheim (see below).

▶ Steelerstrasse is the stop where the
Essen guided buses from Kray rejoin the
street system and operate as normal. This
shows a duo-bus operating in diesel
mode under the tram wires.
M.R. Taplin

▶ The tram subway in Essen where
duo-buses operating in trolleybus mode
share tracks with trams. *M.R. Taplin*

◀ The O-Bahn kerb-guided system must be segregated from other traffic
M.R. Taplin

▼ The piled construction of the concrete guideway is evident in this view.
M.R. Taplin

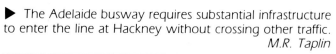

▶ The Adelaide busway requires substantial infrastructure to enter the line at Hackney without crossing other traffic.
M.R. Taplin

ADELAIDE, SOUTH AUSTRALIA

Adelaide is the capital city of South Australia, with a population approaching 1.1 million in the built-up area. The square mile of the city centre is surrounded by parkland and then a huge area of sprawling low-density suburbs. Public transport has been provided since 1975 by the State Transport Authority, controlling six suburban rail lines, one light rail line and about 130 bus routes. The light rail line links the south side of the city centre with the beach resort of Glenelg, and is the surviving link of an extensive tramway system abandoned in the 1950s.

Constrained by hills to the south and east, and the sea to the west, the fastest-growing suburbs are those in the north-east, with a residential population of 100 000 developing over two decades. The increased demand for travel soon placed strains on the road network, with increasing congestion and journey times to the city centre. The River Torrens runs in to the city centre from the north-east, little more than a stream except when in flood, and for years a neglected urban drain. In the 1970s plans were drawn up for a linear park along its course and it was realised this created the opportunity for a north-east transport corridor independent of the road network.

Preliminary designs foresaw the extension of the Glenelg light rail line across the city centre and out to the north east suburb of Modbury (15 km). The project became an election issue in 1980, with the opposition promising a "cheaper" solution, and once they were elected to decision was made to build a busway from Modbury to the edge of the city parkland at Hackney using the Daimler Benz O-Bahn system. Work started in 1982 and the first stage, 6.6 km to Paradise interchange, was opened in March 1986. Government funding difficulties delayed the completion of the outer 5.2 km to Modbury Interchange until August 1989.

The whole scheme cost far more than originally expected, with a total bill of AUD 97.8 million (about £42 million at 1989 prices) made up as follows (AUD million):

    structures 17.0
    alignment 10.5
    guide track 18.9
    stations 16.3
    land 5.8
    landscaping 4.6
    bus fleet 22.0
    services 2.5
    design cost 1.3
    supervision 8.9

An additional AUD 6.4 milion was spent on landscaping not related to the busway.

The outer ends of the routes in the suburbs support only 40-minute headways (hourly off-peak). 10 such routes combine to serve the busway, which has only two intermediate stops, Paradise Interchange and Klemzig, for feeder buses. There are 500 park-and-ride places at Paradise and Modbury. Busway-only peak extras mean 58 buses/hour between Paradise and the city centre at the busiest times. There are 41 rigid Mercedes-Benz 0305 buses and 51 articulated 0305G buses equipped to run on the busway. Once the three-year busway warranty expired, 20 MAN articulated buses were painted in busway colours and fitted with guidewheels to provide back-up. With two serious rear-end collisions occuring on the busway, vehicles are now fitted with rear-end zebra stripes and flashing beacons for use if a bus has to stop for any reason. This illustrates the problem of pretending that buses can be trains that run without signals.

The guided buses run along Currie St and Grenfell St in the city centre, continuing via East Terrace, Rundle Rd and Hackney Rd to the grade-separated junction that marks the start of the busway. There are no special priority for buses along the city streets. Drivers send to draw up some way from the kerb at street stops to avoid the protruding guidewheels striking the kerb, risking damage. The success of the busway in attracting motorists to public transport is its long high-speed run with few stops (use of the linear park means it is quite difficult to take a busway photo that shows any residential properties), compared with the parallel highways which run through a string of local suburban centres. If the busway had conventional stop spacing, and could not be completely segregated, the running time would be little different than on the highway. A study for a busway to serve Flinders University south of the city centre found it would be much slower due to the many level crossings that would be imposed by the flat topography.

THE GLT

In Bristol the Badgerline Group, which owns the Cityline bus company and the Badgerline company serving the city's hinterland, has proposed kerb-guided buses operating on a tidal flow basis over the former Portishead rail line through the Avon Gorge (also the authorised section of the ATA light rail project), but an entirely different guided bus system to serve other areas of the city. This is the Belgian GLT (Guided Light Transit) system developed in 1985 by BN Bombardier, involving a rubber-tyred three-section vehicle that can be steered like a normal bus, or lock on to a single grooved rail for guidance. Electric power comes from an on-board diesel generator, or on guided sections from overhead wire via a pantograph. The Managing Director of Badgerline Rapid Transit, James Freeman, is also involved in the promotion

◀ The busway through the Torrens valley is securely fenced from the adjacent cycle and footpaths. *M.R. Taplin*

▶ The BN guided light transit (GLT) demonstrator vehicle 002 at the Guildhall, Portsmouth on 26th June 1992. *Mervyn Turvey*

◀ Rotherham Corporation Transport had some strange-looking single-ended trams which looked like trolley-buses from the front. Motorists therefore thought that they could swerve and tended to run into them, as this photograph of a battered RCT car No. taken at Templeborough on 15th October 1949 shows. *M.J. O'Connor*

of GLT for the Portsmouth — Gosport — Fareham rapid transit link proposed by Hampshire County Council.

The GLT demonstrator runs on a test track between Jemelle and Rochefort in the Belgian Ardennes, and carried paying customers for a couple of seasons, though this has now ceased. The system by which the guide wheel is pressed onto the grooved rail is said to be excessively noisy. One problem with the GLT when running on its grooved guide rail is that to other road users it will look like a trolleybus which can swerve. This could lead to accidents, as was shown by the single-ended trams in Rotherham which also looked like buses. They were often seen running around with accident damage. Another possible problem with the GLT system if the vehicle is guided by the front section only is the possibility of jack-knifing in poor adhesion conditions. This is a concern of HM Railway Inspectorate and is something which cannot happen to a tram or a kerb-guided bus. No commercial sales of the system have been made.

THE ROLE OF GUIDED BUS

Great Britain seems to be showing the most interest in guided buses at present. A great many studies have been undertaken, if only because promoters of rapid transit schemes have been urged to consider guided buses as another alternative to light rail in preparing their submissions to the Department of Transport. On the one hand these studies can be seen simply as a necessary step towards gaining approval and support for light rail. On the other hand, with the current hold-up in Section 56 finance, certain people have the idea that they might offer an alternative to get a better quality public transport system in place with a cheaper price tag.

Worldwide there has been no great rush to follow the examples of Adelaide and Essen. The only other O-Bahn installation to appear is a section opened in Mannheim. In May 1992 bus route 91 (with a half-hourly headway) started running jointly with trams in one direction over 800 m of Am Aubuckel, serving two stops, and permitting buses to avoid traffic queues on the adjacent highway in the morning peak by using the tramway reservation. Buses in the reverse direction are not held up by traffic congestion and remain on the highway, although trams in both directions (routes 37 and 47 every 15 minutes) are on reservation. Eight new low-floor buses were equipped with guide wheels. The whole project cost DEM 3.5 million, with 85% Federal funding. This is the first guided busway to be worked by low-floor buses, a significant move in view of incrasing social pressures and likely European legislation to make all public transport fully accessible to the mobility impaired. A previous, more ambitious,

Mannheim proposal for a centre to suburbs O-Bahn line put forward in 1987 was dropped in 1990 in favour of a tramway extension.

In fact the Mannheim guideway is the first example of how guided buses may have a future. If a guideway will enable a bus to by-pass congestion bottlenecks, it can make a major contribution towards reducing journey times, restoring reliability, and in deregulated Britain enabling the service to operate at a commercially-viable level with sufficient margin of profit to pay for vehicle renewals. It is this, rather than any wholesale attempt to compete head-on with light rail which should be motivating the bus operators who are showing interest in guided bus technology. The major operators should not be provoking a head-on clash with light rail, if only because they have the opportunity to be involved with the franchise to operate it. Their trade association, the Bus & Coach Council, is at present consdering extending its membership to light rail operators.

Interestingly, of all the vehicle prototypes produced by Daimler Benz for the O-Bahn, the one which no-one has taken up is the 24-metre double-ended articulated 0305G2, designed without manual steering for guideway operation only, and thus confined to the Rastatt test track.

All this means that although it is possible to make a direct comparison between guided bus and light rail on a construction cost per kilometre basis, these comparisons often have little meaning in application. As Dr W. R. Tebb, Group Development Manager of Rider Holdings Ltd of Leeds points out, if 50 per cent of the journey time of a bus is taken up by a congested 10 per cent of the route, installing a guideway for that short section alone will have a dramatic effect on timings and reliability. If, as car ownership increases, a further 10 per cent of the route has to be equipped, that will maintain the improvement. That still leaves 80 per cent of the route where the bus can operate freely on the highway. Meanwhile, this incremental approach to guideway construction gives an immediate payback on a low outlay.

The West Midlands PTE Tracline project, creating a 650-metre long guideway on the former tramway reservation in Streetley Rd to Short Heath terminus, provided an interesting demonstration of the system, but in itself did nothing to ease congestion. It did however form part of a route-enhancement project which included improved information, shelters, traffic priorities and new, specially-liveried, vehicles, and this whole combination produced an increase in passengers of 26 per cent before deregulation.

On the European mainland, one of the arguments put forward in the 1970s for putting short sections of tramway underground was that this incremental approach made immediate use of the assets, even though their full completion as an underground Stadtbahn might be long delayed. In Britain, with buses rather than trams as the starting point, the same argument can now be used for building short sections of guided busway to by-pass congested pinch points. A guideway can be fitted in to road layouts using less space than a conventional bus lane, and where the congestion is at different points in the morning and evening peaks, a single guideway can be used on a tidal flow basis, leaving buses in the other, uncongested, direction on the highway. This is the basis of the Leeds scheme.

South Yorkshire Transport managing director Peter Sephton sees guided busways as a means of restoring reliability and quality to bus services and avoiding them becoming a second class form of public transport alongside the city's £240 million light rail system. The 18 km Sheffield Supertram system will carry 15 to 20 per cent of the city's public transport passengers, but 80 per cent will still travel by bus. SYT is therefore looking at other areas for guided bus and route enhancement projects, including the proposed airport. With Tarmac, Plaxtons and Sheffield Development Corporation, it has commissioned consultants Frank Graham & Partners to study the potential in the Lower Don Valley. (N.B. South Yorkshire Passenger Transport Executive declined to be party to this study). It is significant that the findings of this report have not been made public. This is possibly because the lower Don Valley is hardly an area which has the space problems referred to in the preceeding paragraph. Nevertheless, the study goes out of its way to suggest the conversion of a railway line to guided bus operation. This is rather silly, because where railway track is already in place, it is cheaper to leave the track there and convert to light rail rather than pay the cost of conversion to a road bed, as was found in the Manchester study. Conversely, in the City Centre where there are space problems, the only place where these consultants have managed to find to put their guided busway is in tunnels! Light rail would not need these tunnels, as trams can cross other traffic on the level without losing their guidance system, whereas guided buses cannot.

DISCUSSION

The Frank Graham consultancy submitted evidence on guided buses to the House of Commons Transport Committee in 1991 (see Light Rail Review 3). In its memorandum it said that light rail was most cost-effective where population densities were high, where government policy was inclined towards public transport and where it was incorporated in a public transport policy which favoured integration between modes. Guided bus was said to be 25 per cent cheaper than light rail, with a two-way km cost between £300 000 and £500 000, excluding vehicles. Figures from Adelaide indicate a guideway cost per two-way km of about £2.5 million, excluding vehicles, but this reflects the heavy piled construction that had to be used to overcome unstable clay soil.

If guided bus is regarded as a step-by-step enhancement of existing bus services, cost comparisons with light rail on a whole route basis become somewhat academic. However, it should be noted that evidence to the same Committee quoted two-way km costs for light rail from £1.2 to £2 million, plus £500 000 for overhead power. These are capital cost figures and take no account of life of structures or maintenance costs, which would tip the balance more in favour of light rail because of its 30-year design life. This is one reason why the Section 56 studies showed light rail to be more cost-effective than guided buses in Manchester, Sheffield and Birmingham.

In the same way that light rail is effective in existing rail corridors that can be exploited at low cost, probably the cheapest form of bus guideway construction is where part of an existing roadway can be allocated for busway use by the addition of guiderails. Although Transport & Works Act powers may be sought, this type of construction can be carried out under existing highway authority powers. As soon as special construction in involved, for instance on grassed reservations or new off-road routes, costs will increase, and by a considerable factor where piling has to be used to overcome unstable soil conditions.

Unlike the tram, the kerb-guided O-Bahn cannot be installed for on-street running shared with other traffic, however short the section. This is one advantage of the GLT system with its rail flush with the road surface, and of electronic guidance if it becomes a reality. Unlike tramway promoters, who make sure that all services are moved away from the swept path of their vehicles, guided bus promoters do not accept that it is necessary to go to the considerable expense of diverting services away from the busway, arguing that the occasional occupation by statutory undertakers can be accomodated by temporarily transferring buses to the adjacent highway, even though this means them losing their priority.

One of the most serious problems facing the guided bus is that in itself it does not do much to enhance the image of the bus, which stated preference surveys have found to be consistently down market (a state of affairs rather close to the truth in todays climate of under-investment and fares-based competition). British Rail managers have long talked about ''the sparks effect'', noting that the mere introduction of electrification brings increased patronage. The same has been found when bus routes are converted to tramway operation. The presence of infrastructure creates confidence in the system, its reliability and its function as part of the network.

Such confidence in a system will be needed to make motorists accept it as an alternative to their private cars. The rising costs of traffic congestion are far more likely than environmental considerations to spur the British government into traffic restraint measures and road pricing, although Environment Secretary Michael Howard seems to be making the running over his Transport counterpart John MacGregor, who is on record as saying that new roads improve the environment, and his department will do their bit by makng sure that plenty of trees are planted along them! Motorists will adjust their travel habits only if public transport is available at a quality which matches their car. Light rail provides this quality, but at a rather high initial cost. Faced with the need to limit public expenditure, the Government would love to find a cheaper option, and if this can be introduced in a shorter timescale, so much the better. Is the guided bus the answer?

Operators interested in guided bus now recognise that acceptable public transport means a total package of information (advance and real time), well-equipped stops, comfortable journey, interchange opportunities and ease of use. An informal guided bus group now links Yorkshire Rider, South Yorkshire Transport, Tees & District, Go-Ahead Northern, Newcastle Busways, Hull City Transport, Bus Eireann, Ulsterbus and Badgerline for exchange of views and information. The 1985 Transport Act separated operators from providers of infrastructure and highway facilities, and close co-operation between operators and local authorities has to be established for guided busways to happen. Will a total package of today's technology be enough, particularly if to the general public the buses look little different to those they already know?

One attempt to produce results approaching the light rail effect, but using conventional buses without a guideway, is in Curitiba, Brazil. On several trunk routes continuous bus lanes are provided in what would otherwise be the fast lanes of dual carriageways (flanking the wide central reservation). Specially-built buses have offside doors with floor-height entrances to give level access from matching platforms at stops. Each doorway has plates which drop to meet entrances at shelters built on the central reservation. While the buses look fairly conventional, the stops have been distinctively

◀ The Brazilian city of Curitiba has two corridors served by direct route busways with buses serving special "tube" stop on the medians of wide dual car riageways. Fare collection is by turnstile on entering the station and loading take place through offside centre doors with extending platforms to reach station plat forms.   *EGTC*

designed with tube-shaped shelters, fares are prepaid at turnstiles on entering the stop, and their are self-service lifts for those with impaired mobility. The enhanced image is created by the stop facilities rather than the vehicles.

Inspired by a visit to Brazil, Peter Sephton of SYT has built a prototype "CosyStop". Though not as distinctive as the Curitiba tube, the shelter offers good passenger amenities, including a payphone and real-time information system. SYT would be prepared to pay £10 000 each to install them at busy stops, provided it could be guaranteed exclusive use of them. This is perhaps unlikely when the highway authority has a duty not to inhibit competition: guideways themselves would have to be open to all operators, though whether the low-cost operators with their £5000 second-hand buses would want to spend half as much again equipping them with guideway equipment is a moot point.

Proponents of guided buses argue that with stringently-controlled emissions in new-generation diesel engines, electric traction offers little environmental advantage. Electric traction they claim merely shifts the pollution to the power station (though surely it is easier to control it there than on hundreds of intensively-used individual vehicles). They concede, however, that it may be needed in tunnels. Duo-buses are proven in Essen (except for integration with a subway signalling system), but they carry the weight penalty of two power units at all times. Bus designs achieve their relatively low cost because their major components are derived from units whose development costs are borne by the mass-market truck industry. This advantage is eroded as more and more specialist features in the areas of suspension and propulsion are required.

Bus technology also offers weight advantages. Some recent light rail vehicles have an unladen weight per passenger as high as 225 kg (though novel designs on the drawing board reduce this to 150 kg). The figure for a typical British double-deck bus is 125 kg, and the Daimler Benz 0305G2 guideway bus achives 91 kg. Guided bus developments are a spur to LRV manufacturers to reduce excessive weight and make fuller use of automotive industry components.

Finally comes the question of capacity. The Chartered Institute of Transport's submission to the House of Commons Transport Committee cited flexibility as light rail's key advantage, with a capacity range of 3300 to 20 000

Two views of SYT's 'Cosy stop' taken during a demonstration at Sheffield's Don Valley Stadium. The view from the inside shows the public telephone and the information display.   *Peter Fox*

A Kerb-guidance wheel fitted to an SYT Volvo B10M bus.
Peter Fox

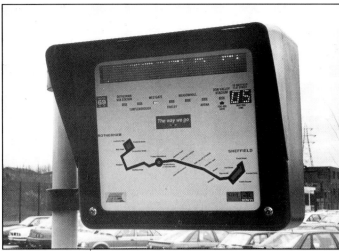

A proposed advance information system which shows where the next bus has reached and the approximate waiting time. Improvements to stops, buses and passenger information systems are surely the way to attract passengers.
Peter Fox

passengers/hour/direction, with greatest effectiveness in the 5000 to 15 000 range. Guided bus's range is given as 2000 to 7000. O-Bahn literature suggests guideway capacities of 16 000, ranging up to 22 000 with articulated buses, but these must be theoretical figures since neither Adelaide nor Essen offer anything like this capacity − indeed one wonders whether a bus every 24 seconds is sustainable in practice! Adelaide's highest recorded peak hour passenger loading is 4285, and the two routes which use the Essen O-Bahn do not even offer this capacity with all seats taken and a full standing load.

CONCLUSIONS

(1) Guided bus systems can be cheaper than light rail systems, but their the costs can rise to be higher than light rail in some circumstances especially when special construction in involved.

(2) The existence of an existing rail right-of-way will favour light rail.

(3) On road alignments, guided bus promoters do not accept that it is necessary to go the the considerable expense of diverting services away from a busway, arguing that the occasional occupation by statutory undertakers can be accomodated by temporarily transferring buses to the adjacent highway, even though this means them losing their priority.

(4) Unlike the tram, the kerb-guided O-Bahn cannot be installed for on-street running shared with other traffic, however short the section.

(5) The GLT system which has its guide rail flush with the road surface can be used for shared running.

(6) The capacity of a light rail system is in the range of 3300 to 20 000 passengers/hour/direction, with greatest effectiveness in the 5000 to 15 000 range. Guided bus's practical range is given as 2000 to 7000.

(7) Light rail vehicles and systems have a 30-year design life, which can make light rail more cost-effective.

(8) A guided bus is no different inside to any other bus, and there is no evidence that motorists would tend to transfer to such a system.

(9) On the other hand, when bus routes are converted to tramway operation, motorists regard the superior layout, quality of ride and generally improved ambience as a real alternative.

(10) The guided bus should be regarded as a step-by-step enhancement of existing bus services, rather than as a serious alternative to light rail.

(11) The guided bus's main advantage lies where part of an existing roadway, too narrow for a conventional bus lane, can be allocated for busway use by the addition of guiderails.

(12) Improvements in bus services are more likely to come from a total package of information (advance and real time), well-equipped stops, comfortable vehicles, bus priorities, interchange opportunities and ease of use, rather than just a guidance system.

(13) The only existing guided bus schemes have been built either because of political considerations (Adelaide) or industry pressure (Essen). No new schemes are being considered in either city.

(14) With capacity claims unproven and public acceptibility in terms of attracting motorists still to be demonstrated, it is too soon to consider the guided bus as a fully-acceptable alternative to light rail over the full range of LRT's capacity and flexibility of application.

ACKNOWLEDGEMENTS

The authors would like to acknowledge assistance from Daimler Benz AG, STA Adelaide, Rider Group, South Yorkshire Transport, J. H. Price and John M. Aldridge in preparing this article. The House of Commons Transport Committee report, Urban Public Transport − the Light Rail Option, is published by HM Stationery Office.

BR SHOWS ITS HAND

A Challenge to the Welsh Office: LRT for Cardiff Bay

by A.W. Elshman

Early in 1993 the Welsh Office will make a decision which, one way or the other, will alter the character of Cardiff, Wales's capital city. The decision to be made is between spending a sum well above £50 million on local roads or on local railways; in effect, the Welsh Office is being asked for the first time ever to treat the local rail system as a transport solution in itself.

Cardiff is a busy, compact city at the heart of former industrial South Wales. Its economy has successfully changed from reliance on the heavy manual work associated with the coal and steel industries to a mix of office work and light industry. Sadly, the same cannot be said of the Valleys to the north, where unemployment has soared since the rapid demise of the coal mines. Now the Valleys people are having to look to Cardiff for jobs, and the Valleys are becoming dormitories for the capital.

The main commuter artery into Cardiff from the Valleys is the A470 road, a dual carriageway over the 24 miles from Merthyr Tydfil to Cardiff's outskirts. Alongside this congested road runs the trunk of the local rail system, branded Valley Lines. Although its tracks are under-utilised, this route plays a significant part in getting Valleys folk to and from work; on the Pontypridd − Cardiff corridor, rail carries 22% of the peak traffic. At present, the roads and the trains are full to capacity at peak times so money will have to be spent increasing transport capacity by the time the ambitious Cardiff Bay development is up and running.

The empty offices at Canary Wharf, London bear silent testimony to what happens when offices are built in a location with inadequate access (by public transport especially). Anxious to avoid the same situation, the developers of Cardiff's former docklands have long since begun work on transport infrastructure. Many millions of pounds have already been ploughed into fast roads around the suburbs; at the heart of the development South Glamorgan county council is building the most expensive road ever funded by a local authority in the UK. £600 000 was given to British Rail for a crossover and new signals at Cardiff Queen Street station to improve Valley Line access to the Bay area via the Bute Road branch.

All this is great news for residents of Cardiff and its suburbs, but the 30,000-job Bay development is also meant to have an impact on the unemployment blackspots in the Valleys. If the Valleys are to benefit at all from the opportunities presented by the Bay development then some way will have to be found to transport workers − in far greater numbers than now − from the Valleys. They will need to travel not *to* Cardiff but *through* it and out the far side, so any solution will have to be closely tied to infrastructure improvements within the city.

The only existing forecasts of growth in travel demand relate to peak-period journeys made by those residents of Cardiff and its suburbs who work in the city centre or in the Bay area. The number of trips currently made in each peak period is expected to double by 2005. This figure came from research by Transportation Planning Associates (TPA) into future demand arising from the Bay development. Sadly, this study was limited to Cardiff and district, and no forecasts are available for the Valleys, for Gwent (to the east) or for West Glamorgan (to the west).

TPA advised a large-scale model transfer from private to public transport, suggesting a target 50:50 split. All the opinions tested by TPA fell short of achieving this target. The best of their options was a guided-bus system (Guided Light Transit) that gave public transport a 48% share. This is likely to be discarded because of its expense.

Now the Welsh Office has commissioned a study on public transport options for the Pontypridd − Cardiff corridor, and BR, via the Welsh Office's consultants, is showing its hand. BR holds an ace − an under-utilised rail system which serves the Valleys and penetrates Cardiff city and the Bay area. After careful consideration, it has decided the best way to play that ace it through Light Rail Transit.

A MIXED SOLUTION

Total conversion of the Valley Lines to LRT is out of the question, at least in the short term, so LRT would have to share tracks with heavy-rail trains, including coal trains. However, BR managers point out that technology now permits safe LRT operation on heavy-rail tracks; in other words, they are turning to the 'Karlsruhe experience'.

Karlsruhe, in southern Germany, has shown how automatic train protection (ATP) permits safe operation of LRT and heavy-rail on the same tracks (see Light Rail Review 1 and 3). This has not passed unnoticed in the UK, where Cardiff joins Nottingham and Tyne & Wear in proposing similar solutions. In spring 1992 representatives of Regional Railways South Wales and West visited Karlsruhe to view its rail systems. They were struck by two things in particular. First was that the combination of LRT and heavy rail gave the region a universal rail option for urban, suburban and inter-urban journeys with no duplication of infrastructure. The second was that Karlsruhe and Cardiff are the same size; the populations of the cities and their respective catchment areas are almost identical.

For the long term, BR managers envisage full electrification of the Valley Lines. Wires would initially cover city-centre routes, Coryton and Penarth lines and the trunk lines as far as Pontypridd and Caerphilly. Electrifying the remainder would sensibly be left until the present Sprinter and Pacer fleet becomes life-expired, when it could be replaced by heavy-rail Electric Multiple Units or further Light Rail Vehicles (LRVs).

THE SCHEME IN DETAIL

To make the initial electrification more manageable, a Phase 1 scheme has been drawn up, taking into account the Welsh Office's desire to relieve congestion on to the A470 trunk road. Under Phase 1, LRT routes would be created between Pontypridd and Cardiff Bay via the City Line and Cardiff Central, and between Cardiff Queen Street station and the Bay. On the Pontypridd line a 15-minute-frequency LRT service

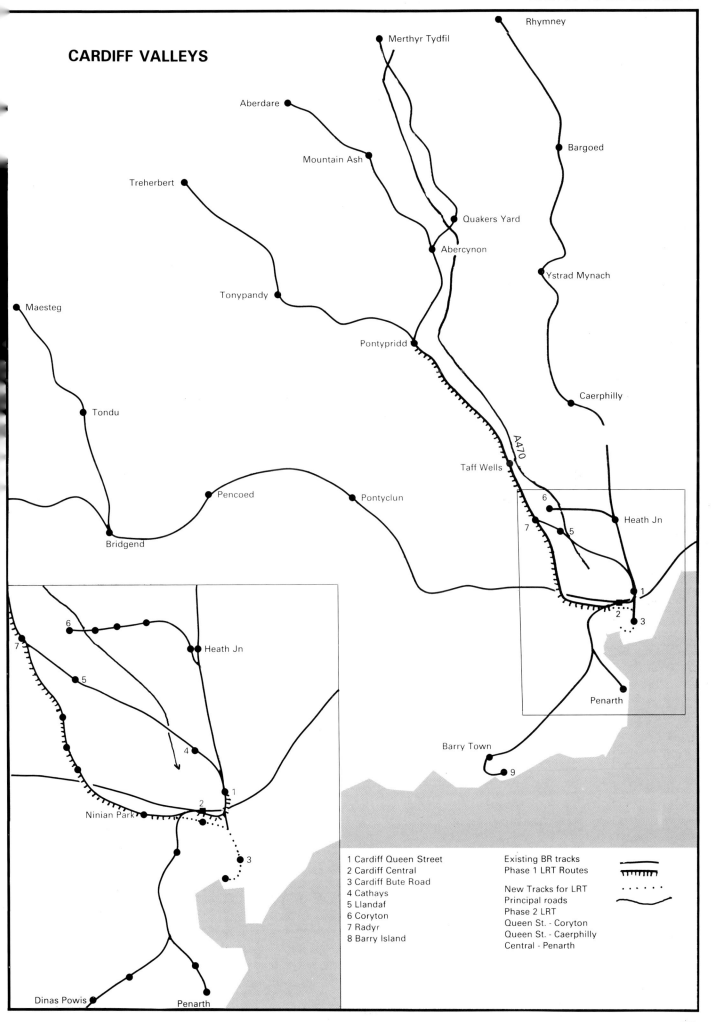

CARDIFF VALLEYS

1 Cardiff Queen Street
2 Cardiff Central
3 Cardiff Bute Road
4 Cathays
5 Llandaf
6 Coryton
7 Radyr
8 Barry Island

Existing BR tracks
Phase 1 LRT Routes

New Tracks for LRT
Principal roads
Phase 2 LRT
Queen St. - Coryton
Queen St. - Caerphilly
Central - Penarth

would be superimposed oN the current diesel service of four trains per hour (two to Treherbert, one each to Aberdare and Merthry Tydfil). The resulting 7½ minute frequency would mean that intending passengers need no longer consult the timetable - an important feature if motorists are to be attracted in large numbers.

The present Bute Road line is carried on a mile-long embankment. Cardiff Bay Development Corporation's desire to demolish this embankment which it sees as a barrier to successful development on land to the east, is one of the reasons why LRT promises to be the most satisfactory solution to all. After crossing over the BR main line to Newport, the LRT Bute Road line would dip sharply to street level — allowing demolition of the problem embankment. With the LRT tracks at ground level, extension of the system to anywhere in the Bay area would be a straightforward matter of laying rails along the street.

For Pontypridd trains to run direct to the Bay a west/south connection between the City Line and the Bute Road line is planned. LRT services would have to call at a separate ground-level part of Cardiff Central station, at the location of the present Riverside station (used until recently by parcels trains). A spacious subway would lead passengers to the LRT from heavy-rail services from the east (Gwent, Bristol, London) and the west (Swansea, Maesteg, Barry).

Initially, 11 light-rail units would be needed to cover eight proposed diagrams — six for the Pontypridd line, two for the Queen Street branch. 28 miles of track would be electrified at £75 000 per single-track. Some four miles of new LRT track are needed, including new graded trackbeds west of Central station and south of Queen Street station. Junctions would need remodelling at Queen Street, Radyr, and Pontypridd, and the embankment carrying the present Bute Road branch would require demolition. Resignalling the Pontypridd line is crucial to the LRT scheme, as is provision of ATP — equipment for which would be fitted to the 35-strong Valley Lines DMU fleet as well as a dedicated set of freight locomotives. LRT stations, power supply and a depot for the LRVs make up the total cost of Phase 1, tentatively estimated at £70 million.

This is an enormous figure for a Welsh rail scheme (although only a fraction of the money being spent of new roads in the area). But against it can be set several costs which would be incurred anyway, namely; resignalling; ATP provision; extra rolling stock; and upgrading the Queen Street — Cardiff Bay line. As all these inevitable costs are encompassed in the Phase 1 package, the cost attribution to LRT provision per se is far less than £70 million.

The Pontypridd line desperately needs resignalling. It now relies on labour-intensive mechanical signalling devised in Victorian days, giving limited headways that do not allow an increase in frequency much beyond the present four trains per hour each way. Some of the signal boxes date back to the pre-1923 Taff Vale Railway, and Radyr is one of the busiest junctions in Britain still controlled exclusively by semaphore signals.

Provision of ATP is also desirable in any case without the LRT scheme. Following the Hidden Report on the Clapham Junction accident, BR was aiming to fit the majority of the

▲ The oversized station at Pontypridd would become the northern terminus of LRT operation. Heavy-rail trains would continue to fork left, for Treherbert, or right, for Aberdare and Merthyr.
R. Clarke

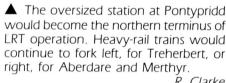

▶ Radyr is where the City line and direct Queen Street lines diverge. 150 270 is seen at the southend of the station with the 13.20 Cardiff Central – Aberdare. *Phil Parsons*

◀ Cardiff Queen Street, the hub of the Valley Lines. The platform on the right is mostly used for services to and from Cardiff Bay area. *R. Clarke*

UK rail network by the early part of the next decade, although funding difficulties are holding this up at present.

The Valley Lines are going to need more rolling stock to cope with increased demand. All but a select handful of peak-period trains are currently formed of unstrengthened two-car units, and the average peak loading is 115% of the trains' capacity — despite a ticket-pricing system that encourages off-peak travel. It is estimated that buying extra stock in the shape of LRVs would cost approximately the same as buying the same number of new Sprinters.

Maintaining the status quo on the Bute Road branch is far from satisfactory from the points if view of both BR and Cardiff Bay Development Corporation (CBDC). If the heavy-rail embankment is retained, contrary to CBDC's wishes, considerable investment would be needed for heavy rail to cope satisfactorily with the huge increase in demand for travel to the Bay area. Double track would need to be reinstated on the branch. Bute Road station itself would be poorly sited in relation to the main Bay development, so some form of heavy-rail extension into the development's heart would be necessary — at far greater cost than LRT penetration. The branch lacks a direct connection to Cardiff Central, so Bay-bound passengers from the Bridgend and Newport directions now have to alight at Central, descend to the subway, ascend at the Valley Lines platform and catch a local train to Queen Street, where they alight again, descend to the subway and ascend at platform three to catch a third train to Bute Road. (The LRT plans would replace this with a descent at Central followed by level access to an LRV direct to the Bay). For a west/south connecting curve for heavy rail, an additional viaduct would be needed — an expensive new structure of the very kind CBDC is trying to banish from the development area.

The Phase 1 LRT project would provide the foundation for a Valley Lines expansion to cope with an increase in demand of up to 360%. Further electrification would allow LRT services to continue north from Queen Street, to Coryton and to Caerphilly, and from Central to Penarth. Within the Bay and the city centre, further on-street or segregated new track could take the LRVs anywhere that is deemed desirable.

THE CHALLENGE

LRT would be a useful marketing tool — for CBDC as well as for BR. The Bay development's success will depend heavily on its ability to attract businesses from continental Europe. Few would be interested in moving to an area accessible only by car and bus, but LRT would be an incentive in itself. The silent, clean operation of modern LRT would convey the image of efficiency and progressiveness that many German, French or Dutch cities can project — but which Cardiff cannot at present.

The challenge facing BR is to encourage commuters and shoppers to forsake the perceived safety, reliability, convenience and comfort of their cars for the railway. A recent survey showed that 75% of regular Valley Lines users felt their train service was good, or very good; people who never used the Valley Lines held them in far lower esteem, perhaps because of bad experiences may years ago. To get them to leave their cars at home or at the nearest Park & Ride station car park, BR must have a product to market which:
(a) looks different to the trains they have in their mind's eye:
(b) runs frequently enough for them not to have to worry about missing trains and not to spend significant periods of their working day waiting for trains;
(c) is fast;
(d) is comfortable;
and (e) takes them where they want to go, not to a station ten minute's walk away.

LRT fulfils these criteria. While heavy-rail expansion would have a limited success — as it has done over the past decade — it would not attract enough motorists to ease current A470 congestion, let alone obviate the need for expansion of the A470 and other roads.

There can be little doubt that combined LRT and heavy rail is the public transport solution for the Valleys, Cardiff city and Cardiff Bay for the next century. It remains for the Welsh Office to choose between the public-transport solution and the private-transport one. 'Between' is the operative word, as investing in one option totally undermines the case for the other. If the A470 is expanded, road travel to Cardiff from the Valleys will be speeded up — removing the Valley Lines' competitive edge. The new, fast roads serving Cardiff Bay will be complete if and when the A470 bottleneck is removed. Currently, the Valley Lines load well where car ownership is low: in the Cynon Valley (served by the Aberdare line) for instance only 52% of households own a car. But car ownership in the Valleys is rising rapidly, and if roads and parking provision continue to increase to match them the railways stand to lose much custom — at least until further congestion forces motorists back to public transport.

Conversely, if money is invested in the Valley Lines LRT Phase 1, rail capacity on the Pontypridd corridor will be

doubled instantly. As the Bay development grows — hopefully in tandem with demand for commuter transport from the Valleys — increasing rail capacity further is simply a matter of buying more trains. And so, with many potential car movements siphoned off by the trains, adding more lanes to the A470 would be pointless.

The arguments in favour of the public-transport option are persuasive. The entire LRT Phase 1 would cost roughly £70 million; adding lanes to the A470 south of Taffs Well would cost an estimated £50million for just ½ mile, because of the Taff Gorge's geographical constraints. A considerable area of prime land in the Bay will need to be set aside for car parks if most of the 30,000 employees are to commute by car; the only prime land the LRT would require is a handful of strips for station platforms (the tracks can run in the roadways if necessary). LRT would also benefit road users; if the railway takes the brunt of the Cardiff commuter traffic, the A470 will be less congested for traffic destined for elsewhere.

Environmentally, LRT has the edge. Occasional LRVs, quiet and fume-free, make for a far pleasanter working environment in Cardiff Bay than a continual procession of cars and buses. LRVs project a more attractive image to would-be investors than multi-storey car parks.

There is no doubt that LRT can be a practical transport solution for a city the size of Cardiff; Karlsruhe has already

proved that conclusively. There is no doubt, too, that buying extra transport capacity would be cheaper through LRT than through a never-ending sequence of road-expansion schemes. But there remains a major obstacle to the LRT plan - a conceptual one rather than a logical one.

For decades there has been no true investment in railways in Wales. The Principality's three new rail services (City Line, Aberdare and Maesteg lines) were produced on such shoestring budgets they can hardly be considered investments in Treasury terms. (Besides, Government funds were not available for the projects, which were funded by local authorities and the EEC). The original Maesteg line scheme was rejected on cost grounds by the Welsh Office, and was only allowed to proceed after it had been pared to its bare minimum — including purchase of second-hand Pacer trains instead of Sprinters. The approved cost was a mere £3.315million.

Clearly, the Welsh Office has always considered local railways as optional extras, perhaps more of political than economic value. Now it is being asked to consider investment in a modern rail system — as an alternative to a major road expansion. Early indications are that it is grasping this alien concept, and treating the rail option as seriously as it has always treated road options, in which case the LRT proposal should shine through on its own merits.

▲ The LRT route would descend to street level at Cardiff Riverside platform shown here in its current disused state. *Phil Parsons*

◄ The end of the line — Bute Road station is uninviting and would be demolished. *Phil Parsons*

WORLD LIST
Urban Tramway and Light Rail Systems 1993
by Michael Taplin

Note: This list excludes museum, rural and purely interurban lines.

* system built new since 1978.
(T) heritage tramway operated primarily for tourist purposes.
Systems in italics are steel wheel, automated, fully-segregated lines.

ARGENTINA

Buenos Aires*.

ARMENIA

Yerevan

AUSTRALIA

Adelaide, Bendigo (T), Melbourne.

AUSTRIA

Gmunden, Graz, Innsbruck, Linz, Wien (Vienna).

AZERBAIJAN

Baku, Sumgait

BELGIUM

Antwerpen, Bruxelles (Brussels), Charleroi, Gent, Oostende.

BOSNIA

Sarajevo.

BRAZIL

Campinas*, Campos do Jordao, Rio de Janeiro* (also T).

BULGARIA

Sofia.

BYELORUSSIA

Minsk, Mosyr, Novopolotsk, Vitebsk

CANADA

Calgary*, Edmonton*, Toronto, *Vancouver*.

CHINA

Anshan, Changchun, Dalian.

CROATIA

Osijek, Zagreb

CZECH REPUBLIC

Brno, Liberec, Most, Olomouc, Ostrava, Plzen, Praha (Prague), Teplice-Trencianske.

EGYPT

El Qahira (Cairo), Helwan*, Iskandariyah (Alexandria), Masr-el-Gedida (Heliopolis).

ESTONIA

Tallinn.

FINLAND

Helsinki.

FRANCE

Grenoble*, Lille, Marseille, Nantes*, Paris*, St. Etienne.

GEORGIA

Tbilisi

GERMANY

Augsburg, Bad Schandau (T), Berlin, Bielefeld, Bochum-

► Latvia's second-largest city, Daugavpils, was closed to most foreigners until the country regained its independence in late 1991. Car 110, a Russian-built KTM5 tram, is pictured at the terminus of route 1 near the railway station, on 10th May 1992. This city and the Latvian capital of Riga are the only cities in the vast former USSR still using trolley poles on their trams, and Daugavpils has the trolley-pole-equipped KTM cars. *S.J. Morgan*

◀ The new Istanbul street tramway is worked by LRVs that have received shielding around couplers and bogies. Because these are high-floor cars, platforms have been built at each stop. Despite running a tram-only contraflow, the LRV is closely followed by a car!   *R. Missen*

◀ The Sirkeci terminus is outside the Istanbul railway station and adjacent to the ferry terminal for the trip across the Golden Horn.   *R. Missen*

▼ A two-car set turns into Divan Yolu at Sultanaimet with St. Sophia's mosque in the background. The line is an excellent link for tourists between terminal/rail station, St. Sophia's, the Blue Mosque and Topkapi palace.   *R. Missen*

Riga (Latvia) has increased the numbers of Tatra T6 cars (officially designated "T3M" in former-USSR cities) in its fleet to at least 60, although the ubiquitous T3 model still dominates the fleet. T6 cars 259 and 260, among the newest examples, are pictured at Centralais Tirgus (Central Market) stop (ending a run on route 2, and now depot-bound), on 12th May 1992. Although Tatra trams operate in several eastern European countries and throughout the former USSR, Riga is now the only city in the world still using trolley-pole current collection on Tatra cars.   *S.J. Morgan*

▶ Riga (Latvia) 901, the prototype articulated tram built in 1989 by the Riga Carriage Works, is pictured west-bound on the Oktobra tilts (bridge) on 12th May 1992. A production run has not followed, and No. 901 remains the only articulated car in Riga's large tram fleet.
S.J. Morgan

Gelsenkirchen, Bonn, Brandenburg, Braunschweig, Bremen, Chemnitz, Cottbus, Darmstadt, Dessau, Dortmund, Dresden, Duisburg, Düsseldorf, Erfurt, Essen, Frankfurt/Main, Frankfurt/Oder, Freiburg/Breisgau, Gera, Görlitz, Gotha, Halberstadt, Halle, Hannover, Heidelberg, Jena, Karlsruhe, Kassel, Köln (Cologne), Krefeld, Leipzig, Ludwigshafen, Magdeburg, Mainz, Mannheim, Mülheim/Ruhr, München (Munich), Naumburg, Nordhausen, Nürnberg, Plauen, Potsdam, Rostock, Schöneiche, Schwerin, Strausberg, Stuttgart, Ulm, Woltersdorf, Würzburg, Zwickau.

HONG KONG

Hong Kong, Tuen Mun*.

HUNGARY

Budapest, Debrecen, Miskolc, Szeged.

INDIA

Calcutta.

ITALY

Genova*, Milano, Napoli, Roma, Torino.

JAPAN

Enoshima, Fukui, Gifu, Hakodate, Hiroshima, Kagoshima, Kitakyushu, Kochi, Kuamamoto, Kyoto, Matsuyama, Nagasaki, Okayama, Osaka, Sapporo, Takaoka, Tokyo, Toyama, Toyohashi.

LATVIA

Daugavpils, Liepaya, Riga

MEXICO

Guadalajara*, Monterrey*, Mexico City.

NETHERLANDS

Amsterdam, Den Haag (The Hague), Rotterdam, Utrecht*.

NORWAY

Oslo, Trondheim.

NORTH KOREA

Pyongyang*.

PARAGUAY

Asuncion.

PHILIPPINES

Manila*.

POLAND

Bydgoszcz, Czestochowa, Elblag, Gdansk (Danzig), Grudziadz, Katowice, Krakow, Lodz, Poznan, Szczecin (Stettin), Torun, Warszawa (Warsaw), Wroclaw (Breslau).

A new tramway system to start public service in 1992 was Konya in Turkey, where Siemens have built a line which is equipped with ex-Köln articulated trams.   *K. Meschede*

PORTUGAL

Lisboa, Porto.

ROMANIA

Arad, Botosani, Braila, Brasov*, Bucuresti, Cluj*, Constanta*, Craiova*, Galati, Iasi, Oradea, Ploeisti*, Resita*, Sibiu, Timisoara.

RUSSIA

Achinsk, Angarsk, Arkhangelsk, Astrakhan, Barnaul, Biysk, Chelyabinsk, Cherepovets, Dzerzhinsk, Grozniy, Irkutsk, Ivanovo, Izhevsk, Kaliningrad, Karpinsk, Kazan, Kemerovo, Khabarovsk, Kolomna, Komsomolsk-na-Amure, Krasnoarmeisk*, Krasnodar, Krasnoturinsk, Krasnoyarsk, Kursk, Lipetsk, Magnitogorsk, Moskva, Naberezhyne-Chelny, Nizhnikamensk, Nizhni Tagil, Nizhni Novgorod, Noginsk, Novocherkassk, Novokuznetsk, Novosibirsk, Novotroitsk, Omsk, Orel, Orsk, Osinniki, Perm, Pro-kopyevsk, Pyatigorsk, Rostov-na-Donu, Ryazan, Sankt-Peterburg, Salavat, Samara, Saratov, Shakhty, Shushenskoye, Simbirsk, Smolensk, Stary Oskol*, Taganrog, Tomsk, Tula, Tver, Ufa, Ulan-Ude, Usolye-Sibirskoye, Ust-Ilimsk*, Ust-Katav, Ustinov, Vladikavkaz, Vladivostok, Volgograd, Volzhiskiy, Volchansk, Voronezh, Yaroslavl, Yekaterinburg, Zlatoust.

SLOVAKIA

Bratislava, Kosice.

SPAIN

Barcelona (T), Soller (T), Valencia*.

SWEDEN

Göteborg (Gothenburg), Lidingö, Norrköping, Stockholm (also T).

SWITZERLAND

Basel, Bern, Bex, Genève, Lausanne*, Neuchâtel, Zürich.

TUNISIA

Tunis*.

TURKEY

Istanbul* (also T), Konya*.

UKRAINE

Avdeyevka, Dnieprodzerzhinsk, Dniepropetrovsk, Donetsk Druzhkova, Gorlovka, Kharkov, Kiev, Konotop, Konstan-tinovka, Kramatorsk, Krivoi Rog, Lugansk, Lvov Makeyevka, Mariupol, Molotzhnoye, Nikolayev, Odessa Stakhanov, Vinnitsa, Yenakievo, Yevpatoria, Zaporozhye Zhitomir.

UNITED KINGDOM

Blackpool, Douglas, Isle of Man (T), *London Docklands* * Newcastle upon Tyne*.

UNITED STATES

Baltimore*, Boston, Buffalo*, Cleveland, Dallas (T), *Detroit* (also T), Fort Worth, Galveston (T), Los Angeles*, Newark New Orleans (also T), Philadelphia, Pittsburgh, Portland* Sacramento*, San Diego*, San Francisco, San Jose*, Seat-tle (T).

UZBEKISTAN

Tashkent

YUGOSLAVIA

Beograd.

Summary: 336, of which 43*.

The Helsinki tramway system is being extended, and soon new low-floor cars will join these 82 Valmet-built articulated trams.   *K. Harris*

SYSTEMS UNDER CONSTRUCTION (11)

BRAZIL Salvador.
FRANCE Rouen, Strasbourg.
N KOREA Daesong.
RUSSIA Togliatti.
TURKEY Ankara.
UK Sheffield.
USA Dallas, Denver, Memphis (T), St Louis.

The latest low-floor cars to be delivered in Germany is a batch of the Kassel type for service on the metre-gauge system in Bochum-Gelsenkirchen.B.A. Schenk

▼ On trial in Torino is this low-floor prototype built by Firema with frame-suspended motors.

SYSTEMS AUTHORISED (13)

BRAZIL Goiana, Belo Horizonte, Joao Pessoa, Teresina.
CZECH REPUBLIC Chomutov.
CHINA Shenzhen.
DENMARK Kobenhavn.
FRANCE Paris, Rouen, Strasbourg.
MALAYSIA Kuala Lumpur.
TURKEY Bursa.
UK Birmingham.
USA Minneapolis, Jersey City.

SYSTEMS PLANNED

These include:

ARGENTINA Cordoba.
AUSTRALIA Brisbane, Sydney.
AUSTRIA Salzburg.
BRAZIL Manaus.
CANADA Victoria.

CHINA Harbin.
FRANCE Amiens, Caen, Lyon, Montpellier, Orleans, Tours.
GERMANY Erlangen, Saarbrücken.
GREECE Athenai.
INDIA Hyderabad.
IRELAND Dublin.
ITALY Bologna, Verona.
MEXICO Tijuana.
NEW ZEALAND Auckland, Wellington.
PAKISTAN Lahore.
SINGAPORE.
SOUTH AFRICA Johannesburg.
SPAIN Barcelona.
SWEDEN Malmö.
THAILAND Bangkok.
TURKEY Izmir, Kayseri.
UK Chester, Cleveland, Croydon, Edinburgh, Glasgow, Leeds, Nottingham, Portsmouth.
USA Chicago, Milwaukee, New York, Norfolk, Phoenix, Salt Lake City, Seattle.

TRAMWAY IN TRANSITION

Melbourne 1992

by Michael Taplin, Chairman, LRTA

Australia's federal capital is Canberra, but this small city is a product of the 20th Century, and one of the reasons for its existence is the intense rivalry between the country's two largest cities, Melbourne and Sydney, respective state capitals of Victoria and New South Wales. Both these great cities are on the coast and built around bays, but whereas Sydney has the most spectacular setting, with its harbour views, Melbourne's coast line is flat and not always easy to find, so the Victorian's claim to the high ground is based on commerce and culture. Melbourne is more conservative than Sydney, and although increasingly cosmopolitan still does not proclaim its attractions in a brash way.

The city's founders were the explorers Batman and Fawkner, who arrived in what is now Port Phillip Bay in 1835, and bought 242 820 hectares of land from the Aboriginals to build a village. Today the greater Melbourne area covers 6110 sq km (more than New York and London put together), with suburbs extending more than 40 km from the central business district. The city has 2.9 million inhabitants, 20 per cent of Australia's population. About 60 000 of these live in the traditional inner city area that was the basis for the development of the southern hemisphere's largest tramway system, now totalling some 220 km of route. About 600 trams run some 22 million vehicle-km to carry around 106 million passengers annually.

TRAMWAY DEVELOPMENT

Melbourne's first tramway was a horse tramway, opened on 20th December 1884 to carry passengers from Fairfield railway station to Thornbury, with the purpose of promoting land sales during the population explosion that followed the Victorian gold rush of the 1850s. However the city became better known for its cable tramway network, promoted by Francis Boardman Clapp, who acquired the patents of Hallidie's successful San Francisco system in 1877. The Spencer Street—Richmond line opened in November 1885 and a 44-mile system was in operation by 1891. Australia's first electric tram was demonstrated at the Centennial International Exhibition in Melbourne in 1888, and the next year a commercial electric tramway was built between the suburbs of Doncaster and Box Hill, opening in October 1889.

Municipal electric tramway systems were developed in the suburbs, and Victorian Railways (VR) built two lines to feed its system. Order came to this rather unco-ordinated development in 1919, when the Melbourne & Metropolitan Tramways Board (MMTB) was constituted to take over all tramways within a 10-mile radius of the General Post Office (with the exception of the two VR lines). This far-sighted move (which may have had an influence on similar moves in London 10 years later) provided a stable authority for the development of a standardised network that forms the basis of today's operation. The last horse tram ran in 1923, and conversion of the cable tramways to electric operation started in 1925. Although the last cable car ran in 1940, the depression, the war and its aftermath meant that the expansion of electric tramways to cover the former cable routes was not completed until 1956.

'THE MET'

The MMTB built no less than 765 standard bogie trams of its W class variants from 1923 to 1956, and these became such a part of the Melbourne landscape that when their numbers started to decline, a campaign was started that led to the survivors being officially listed as mobile historical monuments that cannot be disposed of! The MMTB itself was replaced from 1st July 1983 by the Metropolitan Transit Authority (MTA), formed by the State Government to co-ordinate and operate all public transport in the metropolitan area. This brought the electrified suburban rail system into the same organisation for the first time, with all the benefits of a common fare system, and the whole marketed under the name of The Met. This is still the case today, although the MTA has become the Public Transport Corporation, and is introducing franchising to its suburban bus operations.

One of the significant achievements of the MTA was the implementation of the St. Kilda and Port Melbourne light rail schemes. These two short rail lines from Flinders St. station to bayside suburbs were proposed for closure. With 7000 passengers/day on the St. Kilda line and 3000/day on the Port Melbourne service, revenue averaged 14.5 per cent of operating costs, and the bridge across the Yarra river (dating from 1854) required replacement. The Met plan involved conversion of the lines from broad to standard gauge, changing the electrification from 1500 V d.c. to 600 V, linking the lines with existing tram tracks at Clarendon St. just south of the city centre, and at St. Kilda station and operating through tram services via Spencer St. and Bourke St. in the city centre: 96, St. Kilda Beach — East Brunswick; and 111, Port Melbourne — Exhibition. The new services were inaugurated in November 1987, and their success prompted The Met to propose the conversion of the long Upfield railway line, also heavily loss-making, this time using low-floor cars to maintain facilities for the disabled. However poor public and staff perception of the scheme thwarted its introduction.

City trams.		East Malvern		3	Spencer St-Brunswick St		West Maribyrnong		57
Airport West	59	(Sunday Bus Service*)		377	(Shuttle Service)	30	(Sunday Bus Service)*		357
Bundoora	86	Glen Iris		6	Sth Melb Beach	1	12	West Preston	10	11
Camberwell	72	Latrobe University		87	St Kilda Beach	15	16	Suburban trams.		
Carnegie	67	Malvern		5			96	Footscray-Moonee Ponds		82
Domain Rd-Dudley St	33	Mont Albert	23	42	Sth Melb and	10	12	(Sat pm, Sunday Bus)*		223
East Brighton	64	Moreland	15	22	St Kilda Beach			Northcote-Thornbury		9
East Brunswick	96	North Balwyn	24	48	Toorak		8	Prahran-Nth Richmond		78
East Burwood	75	North Coburg		19	Wattle Park		70	St Kilda Beach-		
East Coburg	1	21	Port Melbourne		111	West Coburg		55	Nth Richmond		79
					(Sunday Tram)		68	St Kilda Beach-Kew		69

▶ A diagrammatic map of the Melbourne tram network.

In 1992, the Swanston Street routes were almost entirely operated by W-class trams, including the last of this type, W7 No. 1040, restored to M&MTB livery. *M.R. Taplin*

1	1	Tram Route Number (City service)
78	78	Tram Route Number (Suburban service)
23	23	Tram Route Number (Peak service only)
357	357	Bus Route Number (Weekends only)

City Tram Route

Suburban Tram Route

Bus Route (Weekends only)

Route continues through intersection

Route turns at intersection

Zone 1

Zone 2

Both Pantograph and trolley-pole equipped trams operate on the same sections of route. A-class car No. 280 is seen passing SW6-class No. 906 in Brunswick Street.

M.R. Taplin

Whereas the MMTB was sufficiently independent to run its own affairs under a succession of strong chairmen such as Alex Cameron, Sir Robert Risson and Dudley Snell, and enjoyed a fine if somewhat conservative reputation, the creation of the MTA inevitably brought a degree of political interference that became more pronounced as various problems of the 1980s manifested themselves. Unionism in Australia is still in the pre-Thatcher era (indeed it is said that many British diehards emigrated to Australia when they saw the writing was on the wall in the UK, and are now active there), and combined with the decidedly confrontational style of Australian politics, plus the evident need to bring budgets under control, the last decade has not been an entirely happy one for Melboune's public transport. The low-point for the tramways was the attempt to force through a new ticketing system and one-man operation of trams, which brought a one-month strike in early 1990, and left both sides to retire to lick their wounds without achieving victory. Happily this nadir of the system's fortunes seems to be over, with more responsible attitudes developing on consultation rather than confrontation, and the lost traffic being won back.

THE SYSTEM TODAY

The European transport professional arriving in Melbourne today will find an expanding tramway system, still operated on rather traditional lines: roving conductors issuing paper tickets validated by hand punches, plenty of inspectors and regulators, most trams with trolley poles, rather slack scheduling, with most routes turning back in the city centre. Much should change over the next few months, with an increased number of pantograph-equipped articulated trams in service, through routeing of most routes across the city, a redefinition of conductors duties and modernisation of the ticketing system. All this will have been achieved by implementing the recommendations of a Ticketing Task Force and a Strategic Review Committee, set up in the wake of the 1990 strike to define an agreed way forward.

The Review Committee report rightly stresses the need to give customers a better service, to be achieved by tram crew workplace reforms, cross-linking of city routes, maintaining an adequate fleet and renewing infrastructure. Better use of traffic management techniques and traffic signal priorities, together with better policing of the Fairway zones to protect trams from traffic congestion will help.

Customer service training is another important suggestion, particularly for conductors, whose jobs should be retained, but widened to stress effective selling and checking of tickets, customer service and assistance (including physical assistance, knowledge of connecting services and tourist attractions, issuing timetables, maps and brochures), keeping the tram clear of rubbish and the collection of survey information. Better training and a career structure is recommended. Ticket-issuing machines to replace the traditional rack and punches will be a significant change. The Committee found that only 84 per cent of the advertised level of service was achieved, due to staff shortage approaching 250 (on a requirement of 2298), leading to overcrowding at peaks, stress and demoralisation. The introduction of cross-city linking would enable a full service to be delivered with just 80 more staff. Reclaiming the 10 per cent of patronage still missing since the strike would bring in AUD 4.2 million/year in revenue.

Running trams across the city centre from one suburb to another is a fundamental part of the plan: proposed new and altered routes are shown on the map. In addition to providing new travel opportunities, cross-city linking achieves major cost savings (AUD 13.3 million/year) by reducing the vehicles and staff required. It will permit the number of W-class trams to be cut from 246 to 111, reducing maintenance and overhaul costs. 10 of the Z-class Comeng/ASEA trams of 1975–79 would be scrapped for component recovery. Better overhaul and preventative maintenance would achieve a saving of 25-30 cars. W-class trams would be retained on routes linking the centre with tourist attractions, but the retained cars will require overhaul and improvement work at a cost of AUD 216 000 per tram.

Infrastructure has been badly neglected for many years, and upgrading is vital if full use is to me made of the fleet of 130 B-class articulated trams now being delivered. An extra AUD 120 million needs to be spent in 1993-97, including reconstruction of 60 km of the 470 single track km on the system, replacement of 170 km of overhead and the remaining wooded traction poles, seven new substations and associated underground cables. Perhaps surprisingly, no rationalisation of the nine operating depots is proposed. New termini layouts are required at the University and in Elizabeth Street to permit more efficient operation and reduce delays. To offset this expenditure, the revenue/cost ratio is expected to improve from 32 per cent to 43 per cent in the first year, and to 50 per cent within three years. Tramway extensions proposed in a 1988 report were:

Airport West–Gladstone Park Shopping Centre (4 km);
Bundoora–South Morang (initial 3 km to Mill Park);
East Burwood–Knox City (initial 4 km to Vermont South);
Mont Albert–Box Hill (2.5 km);
North Balwyn–Doncaster Shoppingtown (3.75 km).

Under construction or authorised by autumn 1992 were Airport West to Airport West Shoppingtown (1.2 km, opened December 1992), East Burwood to Blackburn Road (1.75 km, work started) and Bundoora to Mill Park (by 1995). The report makes the point that all these extensions can be serviced without acquiring additional rolling stock, thanks to cross-city linking. In the longer term docklands redevelopment will give the opportunity to extend Collins Street across the railway, and the St. Kilda and Port Melbourne light rail lines are proposed to be re-routed through the Flinder St station area on the old Yarra bridge.

Reaction to the report has been generally positive, though its formal adoption awaited the result of the state elections which were imminent as this article was written. Predictably the biggest outcry came from the various heritage groups which had succeeded in listing the W-class trams, and saw the proposed reduction to 111 as desecration. The reality is that the PTC has already stored 50 such trams in a North Melbourne warehouse to make room for new deliveries of articulated cars, and would no doubt like to realise their value in overseas sales for heritage tramway projects in North America. Hopefully reason will prevail, though probably not until after the elections.

The October election saw the Labour government replaced by a Conservative committed to saving public funding, and privatisation. In January 1993 it was announced that that conductors would be eliminated, three depots closed, routes 9 and 82 closed, 15 routes replaced by buses after 20.00 hours, and all Met buses sold to private contractors.

Readers will realise that the Melbourne tramway system is unique in many ways, but may be entering an era of great change. With air fares between the UK and Australia at their lowest ever in real terms, now may be the time to go to see a tramway in transition.

▼ The busy Elizabeth Street terminus, serving Flinders Street Station needs a new track layout to ease congestion for reversing trams. Three Z3-class cars can be seen in this view.
M.R. Taplin

◀ Another Melbourne B2-class articulated tram No. 2049, on the St. Kilda light rail line, at the low-platform area of the former Albert Park railway station. The overhead structures date from the railway electrification.   *M.R. Taplin*

▼ The light rail line feeds in to the Bourke Street pedestrian shopping mall.
M.R. Taplin

◀ An articulated B2-class tram No. 2072 en-route to Port Melbourne turns off Clarendon Street with the city centre skyline in the background. *M.R. Taplin*

▶ Melbourne's latest extensions, such as the Bundoora line, have tracks laid in mass concrete. Z3-class No. 216 approaches the terminus. *M.R. Taplin*

◀ A Melbourne conductor goes about his business aboard an articulated tram on its way from Bundoora to the city centre. *M.R. Taplin*

▼ Flinders Street station generates heavy commuter traffic. SW6-class No. 853 and W7-class No. 1021 have arrived from South Melbourne. *M.R. Taplin*

◀ The oldest Melbourne tram in regular revenue service is the 62-year old W2 car 646, driven by staff from South Melbourne depot.   *M.R. Taplin*

▶ A-class car No. 246 carries all-over advertising for naval recruitment and carries the pennant number and name of HMAS Melbourne.   *P. Nicholson*

MELBOURNE TRAMS 1992

Class	Fleet numbers	Built	Builder	Notes
Z1	1–100	1975–78	Comeng/ASEA	All-electric bogie cars
Z2	101–115	1979	Comeng/ASEA	All-electric bogie cars
Z3	116–230	1979–83	Comeng/Duewag/AEG	All-electric bogie cars
L	104/6	1921	James Moore	Drop-centre bogie cars
V	214	1906	Brill	Two-axle cross bench
A	231–300	1984–88	Comeng/Duewag/AEG	All-electric bogie cars
W2	442, 510	1924–28	M&MTB/James Moore	Drop-centre bogie cars
Y	469	1927	M&MTB	Front-door bogie car
Y1	610–613	1930	M&MTB	Front-door bogie car
X2	676	1930	M&MTB	Two-axle, front door
W5/SW5	681–5, 720–849	1935–40	M&MTB	Drop-centre bogie cars
SW6	850–969	1939–51	M&MTB	Drop-centre bogie cars
W6	970–9/81–1000	1951–55	M&MTB	Drop-centre bogie cars
W7	1001–1040	1955–56	M&MTB	Drop-centre bogie cars
PCC	1041	1973	M&MTB/BN	All-electric bogie car
B1	2001–2002	1984	Comeng/Duewag/AEG	6-axle articulated cars
B2	2003–2132	1988–93	Comeng/Duewag/AEG	6-axle articulated cars

L, V, Y, Y1, X2 cars used for tourist duties.
442 and 937 are restaurant trams.
Most W5 cars withdrawn.
1041 is stored.
Museum cars are not shown

PHOTO FEATURE
Developments in France, Germany & Switzerland

▶ The three section verstion of the German prototype VdV low-floor tram (with four axleless wheelsets) has been delivered to Mannheim for trials. *VdV*

◀ Paris is the latest French city to re-introduce trams, on a circumferential route from St. Denis to Bobigny in the northern suburbs. Ten days before the opening of the final section from La Courneuve to St. Denis, driver training was in progress at St. Denis terminus. *David Haydock*

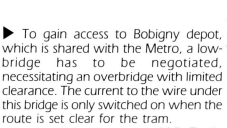

▶ To gain access to Bobigny depot, which is shared with the Metro, a low-bridge has to be negotiated, necessitating an overbridge with limited clearance. The current to the wire under this bridge is only switched on when the route is set clear for the tram. *M.R. Taplin*

◀▲ An interior view of one of Paris's new trams. The seats are more spartan than on the similar Grenoble cars and are of a standard design used on the latest Metro cars operated by the same undertaking, RATP. *Peter Fox*

▲ This RATP bus carries advertising for the new tramway on its front. The slogan reads 'School is cool by tram'. *Peter Fox*

◀ A typical street scene near La Courneuve, the mid-point of the St. Denis – Bobigny line. *Peter Fox*

▼ The existing St. Etienne tram system has had a delivery of new Vevey six-axle articulated cars to replace most of its older cars. New car 908 is seen at the terminus of the recently-completed extension to Hôpital Nord. The new cars look very strange, as they are all fitted with trolley poles. *Peter Fox*

▲ The first system in the former East Germany to receive a new low-floor tram is Halle, whose prototype (built as an add-on to the BOGESTRA order) is seen here awaiting trials in Bochum.
B.A. Schenk

▶▲ Other systems in eastern Germany only have second-hand gifts from western systems. Bielefeld 804 is being prepared for service in Brandenburg, perhaps replacing one of the standard Gotha sets seen on the right.*B.A. Schenk*

▶ Mannheim has created a fleet of accessible terms by adding a low-floor centre to its 1960s Duewag articulated cars.
M. Moerland

▼ Two Karlsruhe dual-voltage trams are seen on the main line between Lausanne and Vevey, Switzerland on 15th September 1992, demonstrating their 'go-anywhere' versatility.
Bernard Collardey

▲**Switzerland.** The roadside light rail line between Zürich, Forch and Esslingen carries increasing traffic since the introduction of a regional tarif system, and more cars are on order to permit increased frequency. Forchbahn cars 202 + 32 + 31 are seen on the 10.48 Zürich – Esslingen in June 1991. *J.C. Baker*

◄ The Bremgarten – Dietikon line is another whose traffic has increased with the regional tarif system. These 1969 articulated cars seen at Wohlen on a local to Dietikon will soon be replaced by a new low-floor design. *J.C. Baker*

▼ The Frauenfeld – Wil line is another totally modernised Swiss rural light rail line. Car 15 is at Münchwilen-Pflegeheim with the 14.33 Wil – Frauenfeld on 18th June 1991. *J.C. Baker*

MANCHESTER METROLINK
Nine Months of Success
by David Holt

Manchester's new Metrolink system has many outstanding qualities, one of which seems to be a knack of loosening passengers' tongues. The talkativeness could have something to do with the novelty of railed street transport to people who previously knew nothing about trams apart from expecting them to have bells. Some folk are still a little confused; one lady was overheard saying "British Rail ought to get some trains like these that you don't have to steer". Be that as it may, whatever stimulates the conversations, the trams' quiet running encourages them. It certainly looks as though the people of Manchester are experiencing the first flickerings of the special affection which trams inspire, and which will surely strengthen with time; a degree of civic pride is very evident in the chattiness, tinged perhaps with a sense of wonder at having been denied such a first-class form of transport for so many years past.

The most common topic talked about on the new system has been the system itself, which is not surprising when one considers how enthusiastically the trams have been welcomed and how quickly they have been adopted as symbols of Manchester. During the Christmas bomb attack on Manchester, the withdrawal of tramway services from the city centre was widely regarded as a key sign of the gravity of the situation, so firmly has Metrolink been adopted as a fixed and fondly-regarded part of the life of the city. By eavesdropping during journeys it has been possible to absorb a whole host of views covering the origins of the project, the height of the platforms, the odd mishap, the frightful closeness with which the trams pass some of the poles, the pros and cons of privatisation, the way the trams share Mosley Street with the buses, the reasons for not yet sharing tracks with trains, and so on until you wish they'd discuss the weather or the ERM for a change. Even so, listening carefully is one way of monitoring public perceptions of Metrolink which are, happily, very positive indeed. When asked how much quicker the tram was than the bus, one passenger replied "Oh, about a day!".

A notable Metrolink fan is the Halle Orchestra's new musical director and conductor, who brought his regard for trams with him from San Francisco. His endorsement counteracts absurd fears that noise from the trams might interfere with performances at the Halle's planned new concert hall near G-MEX, notwithstanding the fact that Amsterdam's Philharmonic Orchestra is based next to a busy tramway junction. Another preposterous bogey was the one raised at a local Green Party meeting, where it was stated that Metrolink "causes pollution by preventing the opening of new railway lines at the cost of enormous pollution from road haulage". Evidently Karlsruhe's operation of trams on DB main lines has not yet been grasped properly.

This report looks at Metrolink's first nine months of operation from the detached point of view of a tramway commuter and city pedestrian.

PATRONAGE

As long as it is reasonably well executed light rail is sure to succeed, and it has certainly done so in Manchester. It is a tribute to GMML and, more than that, to light rail's indigenous excellence and high-street presence that ridership has grown so rapidly. Shopkeepers say that the trams have helped sustain activity at a time of recessionary decline elsewhere. Bury's traders are pleased, and Altrincham's are even more delighted; the local Chamber of Trade and Commerce says that an extra one million people have visited the town since Metrolink opened, and the Greater Altrincham Partnership says that the local housing market has received a distinct boost because of the trams. At 25,000 passenger journeys per day (projected to reach 10 million per annum shortly, yielding a £1 million operating surplus; one million passengers were carried in December alone, in spite of the recession), Metrolink patronage has exceeded the levels associated with the replaced BR Altrincham line and is approaching the popularity of the retired Bury electrics, though still falling short of projections given in GMPTE's 1985 Section 56 grant aid application dating from the times when a significantly larger fleet was anticipated for Phase 1.

An unexpectedly high proportion of Metrolink travel occurs outside the peaks and there are more passenger journeys from end to end of the system than expected, many inter-peak riders being pensioners enjoying publicly-subsidised travel at concessionary fares of 30p each way for any distance. It is clear that some of the tram-riding pensioners are from areas outside the County having no concessionary agreement with Manchester; these people, though they can hardly be expected to know it, are not entitled to concessionary travel. The formula for concessionary top-up from strained public funds is a matter for negotiation and review between GMPTE and GMML, involving accurately-determined factors such as generation and elasticity; an informed exposé of this complex area of public transport funding would be useful. Concessionary fare levels are dependent on struggling Districts' optional contributions to PTA funds. Peak tramway patronage at higher fare levels has been below expectations, which in view of the fare structure is unsurprising. For example, the peak return fare from Timperley (which lies, like Whitefield, at the inner end of a zone) to the city centre is £3.40. City-centre parking, where it is not a free "perk", can be had for £2.50 per day so that for car-owning residents of parts of Timperley the tram can appear pricey though it may be quicker door to door. The bus is not in the same competitive league because its perceived quality is not high enough.

There can be little doubt that generated concessionary travel and GMML's fare structure were initially responsible for spreading demand throughout the day, tending towards the sort of "level playing field" situation which must be the dream of every commercial public transport operator. In the prevailing patchwork of deregulation it is possible that some of Metrolink's optional "grey" patronage has been gained from buses on both competing and different routes. GMML has devised, with the approval of GMPTA/E, a way of meeting the higher-than-expected off-peak demand, which may in time exhibit seasonal variations. From 9th November 1992 the inaugural 12 minute off-peak frequency was doubled by extending the introductory 6 minute peak service to operate throughout the day from 07.30 to 18.30 Monday to Friday, outside which times the frequency is still 12 minutes. On Saturdays, the partial strengthening of services which had already been achieved has been formalised to give a 6 minute service all day between 09.30 and 17.30; outside these shopping hours there is a 12 minute interval. All 6 minute services are

SOLUTIONS....

Metrolink operation and maintenance centre.

Waterloo international terminal approaches – viaduct replacement by bridge slide techniques.

Gatwick airport tracked transit system.

Gloucester Road triangle, Croydon. High speed junction re-configuration to service Inter-Citys' Gatwick Express.

by applying AMEC technology

AMEC Civil Engineering Limited brings together a highly competent group of specialists, to provide the client with the latest systems and methods to ensure cost effective solutions for bridges and trackwork, tunnelling and underground construction, piling and foundations and marine construction specialising in coastal engineering.

Founded in 1883, AMEC Civil Engineering has developed from early bridge work construction servicing the original railway companies, through to providing infrastructure for the automatic guided rapid transit systems for the new developments of both Gatwick and Stansted airports

in the United Kingdom.

Modernisation of structures plus replacing and enlarging permanent way crossings has received the application of our own evolving technology, exampled by the bridge slide technique for under-bridges and ingenious methods to replace overbridges. All developed to ensure minimum disruption to the railway service. The provision of accommodation to the most modern standards, is also a part of AMEC Civil Engineering railway capability. Underground stations, interchanges, maintenance depots, workshops and offices, all required to form a modern and efficient railway service, have been successfully completed.

AMEC
Civil Engineering

AMEC Civil Engineering Limited
Chapel Street, Adlington, Lancashire PR7 4JP · Tel: (0257) 480264 · Fax: (0257) 481801
The AMEC Group

◄ Light rail service on the Bury – Manchester Victoria section of the Manchester Metrolink project was finally inaugurated on 6th April 1992, with early morning departures from both termini, followed by street o0eration between Victoria and G-MEX on 27th April. The first car was No. 1007, carrying the same fleet number of Manchester's "last" tram in 1949, here seen at G-MEX, complete with Manchester Corporation Tramways headboard. *Peter Fox*

▲ The service was extended from G-MEX to Altrincham on 15th June. On 17th July Her Majesty the Queen carried out the official opening ceremony in St. Peters Square. Here she is seen on the rostrum with Councillors Jack Flanagan (left) and Joe Clarke (right). *Peter Fox*

► The Queen is seen enjoying a tram-ride to Bury. *David Holt*

▶ Piccadilly Gardens island platform a
a moderately-busy time on the branch'
opening day, 20th July 1992;
Piccadilly-bound tram has unloaded
crowd of slightly bewildered passenger
from the Bury line onto the inbound sid
of the platform, most of whom are mov
ing across to the outbound side to joir
the next Altrincham-bound tram.
David Ho

▲ Experience in Mosley Street, Piccadilly Gardens is proving that a busy double-decker bus lane is no place for a pair
of facing point switches. With the benefit of pre-sorting (as
shown in the accompanying photograph taken in Rotterdam
in 1985), these switches would have been better located
under 1006's front bogie, with a short length of closely-
interlaced track linking them to the same natural point of
divergence. Various disbenefits have been incurred by the
failure to use pre-sorting techniques for all three of Manchester's sets of powered on-street points. The Y-points in
Parker Street would with pre-sorting have been much less
prone to derailments, and in Market Street a pre-sorting arrangement would have made it possible to improve the rear-
end swept path of Direct trams as well as keeping the switches clear of any future Tib street bus lane. The particular
set seen in this photograph is suffering greviously in the
wheel-path of hundreds of heavy buses, so much so that the
points' mass detector coil has had to be roofed over with
wood for protection. *David Holt*

▶ A typical example of modern pre-sorting tramway points;
these form part of a turning loop at Station Blaak, Rotterdam.
David Holt

characterised by alternate ''Direct'' workings avoiding the
Piccadilly branch.

16 extra drivers were recruited to cover the extra workings; it was their training which delayed inauguration of the
improved services — and aggravated the predictable autumn
increase in wheel-flatting, a problem which now seems to be
diminishing again. Some peripheral benefits of the improved
frequencies deserve mentioning. By-passing of the Piccadilly branch by alternate workings has improved things for
through travellers. More units on the line means more electrical receptivity and this in turn means a higher incidence
of regenerative braking, potentially leading to better overall
energy efficiency. The extra units in and around the city have
intensified transit presence and awareness, potentially leading

both to greater safety and to increased ridership. And, finally, for those needing to photograph or film the trams, the increased frequencies mean less hanging around between shots.

Off-peak passengers obtain even better value from the
unaltered fare structure, offering for the same reduced price
a service twice as good. Meanwhile delivery of the advertised peak 5 minute frequency is being postponed again. Assum-
ing no peak operation of coupled pairs, full provision of the
5 minute service featured prominently up to and during the
tendering process would require 23 vehicles out of the present 26 to be available morning and afternoon. It is obvious
that the retained introductory 6-minute service, requiring only
20 vehicles, is much better matched to the present 26-vehicle
fleet.

The arrangements outlined above were put in place for a trial period of 6 months. It is possible that the extra ridership generated by the enhanced off-peak services will spill over into the evening peaks, during which crush loadings are already experienced, especially during school holidays; the writer travels home most evenings by tram in packed conditions. Passengers are often obliged to wait for the next tram, while traffic congestion persists on parallel roads. If over-crowding in the evening peaks becomes a serious problem GMML may strengthen services by the operation of some coupled pairs though it has to be said that this could only be done on a limited basis with the present number of vehicles. Ultimately it is hoped that increasing levels of patronage will bring forward the acquisition of extra vehicles so that coupling can be achieved to the extent foretold during the scheme's promotion.

TICKETS

Fares are being maintained at their inaugural levels for the time being. GMML is anxious to add banknote acceptors to the ticket machines and is planning a pilot scheme covering some of the bigger stations, a major difficulty being reliability with damp or damaged notes. There is a possibility that extra ticket machines may be fitted at some stations where experience has shown a need for them, for example on the inbound platform at Stretford. GMPTE proposes a county-wide "Smartcard" ticketing system, which would include Metrolink. The PTE is also planning a ticket sales facility with a shop front in the city-centre; tickets will be available for all public transport travel within the County, including Metrolink. Meanwhile the low incidence of fare evasion and the high standard of public behaviour on the tramways reflect credit on GMML's popular Customer Service Inspectors working in light rail's open environment, backed by a tram-riding civil police team. Women find Metrolink so secure that it has opened up new travel opportunities for them in the evenings, though it is unfortunate from the point of view of personal security that a handful of drivers lightly increase their isolation from passengers by closing the cab partition blinds;

on a conductor-less system this prejudices a very important fringe benefit of LRT — its openness. Enough drivers manage without the blinds to suggest that their closure may be a matter of preference rather than necessity.

TRANSIT PRIORITY

Traffic signal delays to Manchester's trams normally last only a few seconds, so that the passenger's perception of a ride through the city is one of smooth unimpeded progress. That is not to say that all the signals have been working well. For example, inbound trams have persistently been forced to a standstill by the LRT signal at Princess Street with the bus signal at green and the conflicting traffic stationary, and it must have been tempting for drivers to pass the Peter Street LRT signal when, similarly, it was showing "Stop" and the adjacent traffic signal was showing green and there was no conflicting traffic. Between lights it is extremely rare (in fact, in the writer's experience, unknown) for a tram's path to be obstructed by parked road-only vehicles; other drivers are obviously learning to respect the imposing trams with their protruding couplers.

SUNDAY SERVICES

Continuing civil works initially forbade Sunday operation. However, on 4th October a limited Sunday service was started between Altrincham and Piccadilly in connection with the termination from that date onwards of BR's Sunday Chester trains at Altrincham. At first the trams operated half-hourly between 12.54 and 23.25 hours to meet the trains, tickets from stations beyond Altrincham being valid for through tram travel to Manchester. With sufficient advancement of work on the Bury line's Besses o' th' Barn bridge, a full 15 minute Sunday service was put in place from 15th November throughout the Phase 1 system. Sunday patronage is building up well in response. Manchester's last completely tramless Sunday morning — 8th November — coincided with the annual Remembrance Service at the Cenotaph adjacent to St Peter's Square, where GMML's laying of a "Metrolink" wreath recalled the many "Tramways" wreaths once laid at Cenotaphs in various

▲ The emergence of trams at speed from Piccadilly Undercroft is heralded only by silent "wig-wag" signals, one of which is visible here; no mirror has yet been provided to allow tram drivers and pedestrians to check for each other's approach. No. 1025 is seen leaving Piccadilly Undercroft.   *Peter Fox*

◄ Car 1005 leaves Mosley Street station for G-MEX on opening day. Mosley Street is one of the 'profiled platforms' referred to in previous editions.*Peter Fox*

3ritish cities.

CHRISTMAS CARE – "DONT DRINK AND DRIVE"

During the festive season Metrolink made a truly worthwhile contribution to the "Don't Drink and Drive" campaign by extending its tram services, with the support of the Bass brewing company, until 01.00 on Christmas Eve and New Year's Eve. In addition, fares were reduced in off-peak periods during Christmas Week – the writer was delighted to be charged only 90p return tram fare against an equivalent bus price of £1.90. No untoward incidents marred the late night operations, and at least one driver was given a standing ovation by good-natured revellers. Will other public transport operators follow Metrolink's example?

THROUGH FARES

British Rail is working on plans to offer through booking from any BR station in the UK to Metrolink and return, though this is unlikely to be in place before May 1993 for ordinary tickets. Through booking will be possible only from British Rail stations; it would not be feasible for Metrolink's ticket machines to cope with hundreds of BR destinations, though the presence of some sort of ticket-sales facilities in the city centre might be a useful marketing tool for BR. Meanwhile the attractions of Metrolink are being put to good use by BR through the promotion of tramway connection possibilities in new train timetables. Through a PTE initiative train tickets bought within Greater Manchester for travel into or across the city are valid within Metrolink's city centre zone; this means that outbound Metrolink commuters paying full commercial rates have to compete for space with PTE-subsidised passengers.

GMML continues the difficult pursuit of through bus/tram ticketting, hampered by the fragmented state of local bus administration (76 operators at the latest count, aggravated by a three-way split of GM Buses threatened for 1993) in the persisting deregulated environment. These and other factors, such as the postponement of new park-and-ride initiatives and the unfortunate concealment of the tramway behind redundant station buildings, are conspiring to suppress Metrolink's true demand potential; there is no doubt that the tramway traffic offered would far overwhelm Phase 1's initial fleet capacity if all restraints were cast aside, as they will surely have to be if road pricing ever comes into force. Metrolink's capacity has, indeed, already being dramatically overwhelmed on at least one particular Saturday. Until the fleet is enlarged we must be content with a fundamentally sound infrastructure investment which has yet to be used to carry the number of vehicles needed to exploit it to its full potential.

PICCADILLY

Perhaps the most contentious Metrolink development was the change in service patterns brought about by the opening of the Piccadilly branch on Monday 20th July 1992. Until that time, all trams operated "Direct" – that is to say they ran from Altrincham to Bury via G-MEX, Market Street and Victoria. After 20th July, most ran via Piccadilly Station. Through passengers found themselves having to change cars to continue their journeys across the city – unless they were lucky enough to be on one of the alternate peak-hour through workings. Confusion abounded. Many intending passengers travelling towards Altrincham and boarding at (for example) High Street mistakenly waited for a tram displaying "Altrincham", unaware that the drill was to board one showing "Piccadilly" and change at Piccadilly Gardens. The situation has been eased by the newly extended 6 minute service with its alternate "Direct" and "Piccadilly" workings.

Initial consternation was offset a little through guidance given by customer service inspectors (CSIs), controllers and drivers though the absence of destination displays on the sides of the vehicles has been acutely felt throughout the system. Neither was the situation helped by the whimsical way in which some of the system maps show the branch attached to the wrong side of the through line. Relatively few passengers seemed to welcome the Piccadilly deviation, having been spoilt by the initial "Direct"-only services. The upset was at its worst in the earliest days of the branch, things having improved considerably since.

Strenuous efforts are now being made to ensure that good connections are made at Piccadilly Gardens, though there are still exceptions. When punctuality is backed by adequate information, as is increasingly the case, it is painless enough – and quite impressive – for through passengers to transfer immediately to an outbound vehicle waiting at Piccadilly Gardens island platform with its doors open. Before the introduction of the inter-peak "Direct" workings there were calls for through passengers, especially disabled people, to be allowed to remain on board during the excursion down the branch and back again. Passengers cannot, however, be allowed to remain aboard beyond the undercroft's terminal platforms and into the headshunt area; certain details of the reversing arrangements would first have to be modified to the satisfaction of HM Inspecting Officer of Railways. It is surprising that no compulsory stop has been imposed for safety reasons on the trams where they emerge directly from the undercroft to cross a busy footway and London Road itself. Operation of coupled pairs down the branch is awaiting the provision of additional emergency exits in Piccadilly undercroft. Aytoun Street crossover has seen occasional use.

▶ Beneath BR's Piccadilly station, Metrolink's trams call at platforms boxed in by thick concrete barricades designed to prevent any contact between the trams and the cast iron columns supporting the main line station. The pathway in the foreground links Fairfield Street with the outbound platform; the tram is waiting to move forward across London Road *en route* to Bury.   *David Holt*

◀ On 21st July 1992 a complete service of coupled sets, seven in all, operated between Altrincham and Victoria in connection with the 'Simply Red' concert at Old Trafford cricket ground. Here is No. 1010 "Manchester Champion" forming the front half of a coupled pair at Old Trafford station bound for Altrincham.   *David Holt*

THE TRAMS THEMSELVES

It is instructive to reflect on some of the design features of Metrolink's fleet of trams, the nature of the DBOM contract having made it unlikely that every design imperfection would be avoided in the impressive light rail vehicles. In general terms the trams look good and feel incomparably better to ride on than anything else on the road, demonstrating that trams represent the supreme commitment to public transport. Having said that it would be negative to ignore the few flaws incorporated in defiance of the abundance of accumulated tramway wisdom which was available from home and abroad. The external feature of the cars which most worries passers-by is the rear-end outswing with its low-level leading edge which comes startlingly close to pedestrians on the outsides of curves in the city centre. A related comment has been made about the livery. When viewed from the side, the extremely pale principal colour closely matches the colour of cleaned-up concrete or Portland stone buildings. This produces a camouflage effect which is of special concern to partially-sighted pedestrians approaching the sides of vehicles which might throw out their back ends unexpectedly on curves. Those who must mingle with the trams in the city centre might have preferred the orange livery proposed by GMPTE, though this was not the only factor which had to be considered by GMML's design consultants.

It is very difficult to understand why Manchester adopted whistles for on-street use instead of specifying conventional power gongs. One theory about Manchester's exceptional spurning of gongs is that they were thought to impose a "down-market" image in the contorted sense of people being thought willing to pay more to ride on "trains" rather than on "old fashioned" trams; gongs, like nothing else, would indelibly label the vehicles "trams". Even so the Manchester public, in spite of efforts to persuade them otherwise, have persisted in proudly referring to their new vehicles as "trams". To the writer's ears the whistles speak clearly only of a crass old 'sixties stigmatisation of trams dismally inappropriate on a brand-new tramway system.

So what's wrong with the whistles? At a much louder volume they might suit the Canadian Rockies or Shap but they do not have the "attack" or "edge" so vital for street use. Gongs, on the other hand ring out a distinctive sound of impact to attract attention sharply but not annoyingly; that is why street-operating rail vehicles all over the world have always been, and will always continue to be, associated with a bell sound. Television has led people to expect gongs and

it is perverse to insist otherwise. We may have to wait fo the arrival of Sheffield's gong-equipped Supertrams before the message takes root from the other side of the Pennines a glaring reversal of the old adage "What Manchester doe: today, others do tomorrow". Every tram driver is glad o a gong; denied their benefits, a few Metrolink drivers broad cast the unfitness of the variously-toned whistles by frequently activating the piercing horn fitted for high-speed off-street use

To sound the loud horn in the city-centre, the whole vehicle has to be put into off-street mode. The driver must reach behind him to rotate the running mode selector switch with his right hand before sounding the loud horn with his left thumb, after which he must remember to restore the selector switch to the correct one of its two on-street positions. This ergonomically ghastly procedure may take place when moving towards threatening situations in the city centre. The selector switch is rotated using the same right hand which, one might think, ought to be ready to initiate an emergency stop by striking the magnetic track brake button in the centre of the main console.

As it is, ill-will can too easily appear to lie behind the high-speed horn's use in the city centre, most of which is directed at baulked buses right outside GMPTE's headquarters offices on Portland Street — which is ironic because that is where

▲ The best views forward from Metrolink's trams are obtained from the gangway seats nearest the front, so much so that many passengers are reluctant to move across when the tram fills up. *David Holt*

◄ The lack of grab-poles in the aisles of Metrolink's trams results in clustering of passengers in the door lobbies, as shown to a mild degree in this on-board scene. These cubs, beavers and scouts from Disley are enjoying a Saturday tram ride to the East Lancashire Railway at Bury. *David Holt*

he decision to adopt the inadequate soft whistles may very well have been made. Three particularly bad examples of the off-street horn's use spring to mind, each of which was regretfully witnessed by the writer; in one case the loud horn was blasted at to an elderly lady who didn't move quickly enough out of the tram's path, in another case it was used for no good purpose late at night outside a hotel and in another it was directed against a properly-behaved car driver at a box junction. On such occasions, Metrolink's discourteous horns scream out to all and sundry that the soft whistles can't do their job.

ON-BOARD FACILITIES

With its splendid degree of accessibility Metrolink is spearheading the trend towards banishing lowly discrimination on the grounds of disability or encumbrance. The provision of obstruction-free access to a mass transit system is fraught with all kinds of problems, to which Metrolink is responding as far as is humanly possible. GMML's Chief Executive who himself is in the process of qualifying to drive the trams, meets on a regular basis with representatives of people with various mobility problems as well as other transport users; these meetings are also attended by GMPTA/E members and officers. Metrolink's heart-warming commitment to the almost impossible, but eminently worthwhile, task of catering for every member of the community has favourably impressed the Olympic Selection Committee, currently evaluating Manchester's bid to host the 2000 Olympic Games; the successful contender will also host the Paralympics and each bidder has to demonstrate an ability to cater properly for disabled people. Thanks to Metrolink, Manchester is in an excellent position as the only bidder boasting a fully accessible mass transit system. As well as supporting Manchester's Olympic bid, GMML has underlined its commitment to the community by adopting Christie Hospital as the official Metrolink charity. Car 1025 has been named the "Christie Metro Challenger".

During the short life of the system so far, the trams have had to cope with all manner of loadings ranging from 500 souls aboard a coupled pair of trams, to sudden influxes of wheelchairs or of parents accompanied by youngsters in buggies or toddling on foot. One of the oddest sights on the trams must have been a couple of wildfowling buffs perched on their shooting sticks in a door lobby, each having a tame hawk on his gloved hand. Well, there's no bye-law against it! Tens of thousands of passengers have had to learn how to make the best use of on-board facilities and how to exercise proper regard for the needs of others. On the multi-accessible system, drivers have also had to bear in mind the special nature of their human cargoes, which might be thought of as so many loosely-packed eggs. It is, for example, very easy for poorly-supported passengers to fall onto the occupants of baby-buggies if trams are accelerated too fast out of sharp oddly-shaped bends in the track; Metrolink does, however, provide a remarkably comfortable ride largely free of nasty dynamic events. The traction and service braking dynamics are generally impeccable.

The lack of grab-poles and hand-straps in the narrow aisles causes clustering of passengers within the door-lobbies. People dislike raising their arms to reach the handrails fitted above the seats, which are too high to draw passengers voluntarily "down the car". This gives an ironic twist to one of GMML's advertising slogans "Don't get long arms — get the Met". Similarly, there is a subconscious reluctance to intrude on others' space by using seat-back hand-holds. Nevertheless, passengers do respond willingly when drivers once in a while ask them to "pass along the aisles please". This alleviates doorway clustering which otherwise obstructs a high proportion of alighting passengers as well as giving a false impression of capacity loading at stations even though the vehicle

may be carrying only half its true complement of standing passengers. When on the other hand standees are cajoled along the aisles, their presence against the cab door can make it impossible for the driver to exit rapidly from his cab. Gangway grab-poles and hand-straps, if provided, might be omitted from the two seat bays nearest the cab doors so as to keep standees clear of them most of the time, maintaining as far as possible drivers' ease of egress from the cab. There are no external cab doors.

The space provided for wheelchairs, luggage, baggage and standees adjacent to the door lobbies is proving popular and useful. The variety of items brought on board has been as amazing as it is on any multi-access system; there have even been examples of bicycles being conveyed in contravention of the byelaws. One interesting diversion for drivers has been to be gurgled at by infants over the intercom provided for the use of disabled passengers, the communication panel being at just the right height for tiny tots in trollies. For seated passengers, the design of the cab partition windows means that access to empty window seats near the front may be obstructed by forward-gazing occupants of gangway seats, from which the view forward is better than from the window seats. Throughout the trams the placing of baggage on seats is commonplace enough to need "please clear all vacant seats!" announcements from drivers as new passengers board crowded trams. Conversion to 2 + 1 seating would alleviate the problem as well as bringing the trams more into line with European practice, dramatically — though controversially — increasing capacity at minimum cost.

FUTURE DEVELOPMENTS

The Government's under-commitment to public transport is, together with the slow bursting of the 'eighties economic bubble, delaying Metrolink's growth though GMPTE has won widespread Parliamentary powers and is submitting an application to the Government for funds to convert the Oldham/Rochdale line to LRT, with on-street penetration of the centres of both towns. The response is anxiously awaited; a quick go-ahead would allow services to be started in two or three years' time; the requisite legislation has already been enacted, as it has for other extensions.

Some time ago, when it appeared that any new LRT route relying on public funds was unlikely to go ahead in the immediate future, a radical review of extension plans was undertaken. Trafford Park, Salford Quays and Rochdale/Oldham were the favourite survivors, added to which there has been talk of new tram routes to the University and Hulme, Manchester Airport and Wythenshawe, and the Eastlands Olympic site and Ashton. Discussions are continuing with developers in Trafford Park and Salford Quays, both of these extensions being expected to attract private funding. Oldham/Rochdale has already been mentioned. Another possibility is an extension beyond Altrincham to link with a Park and Ride facility on the M56.

CONCLUSIONS

What we have in Manchester is a light rail installation which has quickly become popular because of the tram's positive qualities, uniquely combining the "pull" of electricity with the subconscious appeal of shiny steel rails dependably linking the heart of the city with its suburbs. Metrolink Phase 1 is successful because it is a well-conceived modern tramway system linking two well-used commuter railways; leaving aside extensions for the moment, it now needs a package of measures to make fuller use of the excellent investment it represents. First of all the highest fleet number needs raising by fleet expansion from 1026 to 1036, 1046 or 1056. At the same time, the notoriously gruesome traction pole count in the city centre ought to be reduced urgently. One or two extra stations are needed on both lines to serve more residential

◀ Occasionally Metrolink's capacity i stretched to the limits, as this Saturda scene at Stretford station shows. Thes people had listened to a series of PA an nouncements telling them not to try t board one crowded inbound tram afte another. Several finally gave up, one man was embarrasingly told off by disembodied voice for daring to seek in formation via the emergency call point while others ultimately forced their way aboard. Conditions like these prolong stop dwell times, further reducing line capacity. *David Hol*

▶ At Old Trafford station after the Simply Red concert held on Saturday 18th July, Amanda Best, senior controller, waits at the controls of 1024 while Tracy Hadfield, Customer Service Inspector, shepherds homegoing concertgoers aboard this coupled pair of trams bound for Victoria at around 22.15.
David Holt

▼ When trams don't stop accurately at Metrolink's profiled platforms, passengers are faced with a considerable door sill to platform height discrepancy. This car is operating singly and so the sliding step has not been activated. *David Holt*

areas. Some inherited station buildings need demolishing so as to end their outdated reign as barriers segregating the vibrant new transport system from the public domain. More widespread signposting is needed. A handful of design bugs and omissions need to be sorted out to refine the system and make it friendlier. A strategic Park and Ride facility is needed for each line and the effects of the sharpest per-kilometre fares peaks — such as Timperley to G-MEX and Whitefield to Victoria — ought to be alleviated in some way; for example, the manually-sold period passes could be priced on a strictly per-kilometre basis. All these measures, applicable only to Phase 1 (Bury to Altrincham), could add up to a dramatic increase in ridership above the levels predicted in GMPTE's 1985 submission to the Government for Section 56 funds to build the system. One day soon perhaps Metrolink will surpass the expectations of those brave days, but for now we must be glad that a splendid introductory sample of light rail is on the ground in caring and capable hands, a valuable civic asset in need of early expansion to build on success and to further exploit the abilities of a superlative form of transport which is earning a singularly fine reputation amongst Mancunians for comfort, reliability and punctuality.

LIGHT RAIL TRANSIT

Current Developments in the United Kingdom

by Michael Taplin

The period since the publication of Light Rail Review 3 has seen the final commissioning and opening for public service of the Manchester Metrolink, Britain's first modern light rail system to feature street operation, and substantial progress with the construction of Sheffield Supertram. However these positive developments have been overshadowed by political and economic developments that have cast a pall of gloom over all those involved with the promotion of public transport projects.

Suggestions at the turn of the year that the recession was bottoming out, and the first green shoots of recovery could be detected, have proved to be mere political rhetoric, but were perhaps sufficient to sway the floating voter to the extent that the outcome of the British general election in April 1992 was the return of a Conservative government for a record fourth term. The election campaign saw considerable differences between the main protagonists about the direction of transport policy, though whether the true economic situation would have made the subsequent reality very different whoever had won can only be speculation. At least the Labour Party was committed to a programme of public investment in infrastructure products, which would have seen further progress with light rail schemes as well as much-needed improvements in bus public transport.

As it was, the consequent Ministerial reshuffle saw all but one of the transport team replaced, and a new Secretary of State in John MacGregor, who had no time to make his mark before suffering the iron rod of the Treasury on any expenditure plans he may have had. On 8th June he announced that there would be no additional funding for light rail schemes beyond the £50 million a year already committed. Since the Sheffield Supertram project took up all of this funding in 1992/3 and 1993/4, it would not be possible to make a Section 56 grant to permit work to start on line 1 of Midland Metro, even though the project met all the criteria for grant. The additional resources could not be found for 1993/4 and this reflected the need to control public expenditure in the light of prevailing economic conditions.

The surviving member of the Ministerial team is Roger Freeman, who remains responsible for public transport outside London, and has made enough encouraging remarks about light rail to be regarded as favouring investment in these projects if national resource constraints permit. Transport in London is the responsibility of Stephen Norris, who has made favourable remarks about the Croydon Tramlink scheme. Clearly the rapid worsening of the economic situation in the second half of 1992, including the effective devaluation of sterling against major European currencies by over 10 per cent, means that most areas of public expenditure will be cut in 1993/4. It remains to me seen whether October's traumatic political developments, with an apparent commitment to maintaining infrastructure projects that secure employment, will bring any benefit to major public transport schemes.

All this emphasises how urgent is the need to find alternative funding sources for public transport infrastructure projects. There are no shortage of examples: road pricing in Norway, petrol tax in Germany, local payroll tax in France, benefit taxes in Canada, local sales tax and bond issues in the USA. The option of doing nothing should not exist for a government which made environmental commitments at the Rio de Janeiro Earth Summit recognising that the growth in vehicle exhaust gas emissions is unsustainable.

In the meantime the MacGregor announcement has put the damper on many other politicians' aspirations for light rail in their own areas, and many British cities that were promoting schemes have put their plans on hold, or downgraded them to improved bus systems in the short term. The civil engineering and railway vehicle manufacturers have also had to revise their forecasts of the work available in the future: for instance GEC has disbanded its Transportation Projects subsidiary. It is ironic indeed that following the bankcruptcy of the Italian SOCIMI company, the ABB group has decided to have the mechanical parts of the advanced tram design for Strasbourg built at its Derby (ex-BREL) plant.

The year has also seen the passage of the Transport & Works Act on to the statute book, which means that light rail schemes are no longer authorised by private Acts of Parliament, but by Orders made by the Secretary of State for Transport (after a local public enquiry) in a similar manner to road schemes. 1991 Bills to authorise light rail proposals are still in Parliament, and cover Croydon, Leeds and Nottingham for new schemes, and London Docklands, Manchester, South Yorkshire and the West Midlands for extension/amendment of existing schemes.

City by city developments since the publication of Light Rail Review 3 are described below.

AVON

The privately-promoted scheme for a light rail system in the Bristol area has ground to a halt with the company Advanced Transport for Avon Ltd running out of funds, and being wound up in October 1992. The joint venture project with Avon County Council has ceased therefore, and the County is now carrying out its own study of rapid transit potential, including evaluation of light rail in comparison with the guided bus and GLT options put forward by the Badgerline group, and an economic evaluation of the 51 km light rail scheme. The County Council anticipates spending £1.8 million on preparatory work before seeking Orders in 1993−4. In the meantime the results of the city centre study (which led to Parliament rejecting ATA's central area Bill as premature) have confirmed that the original route proposed was the best initial option, and this has been accepted by Avon County Council and Bristol City Council. In addition to GLT, Badgerline Rapid Transit is promoting the conversion of the Gordano−Wapping Wharf rail alignment (also covered by the ATA Act of Parliament) to a busway for tidal flow with kerb-guided buses. The new Cribbs Causeway out-of-town shopping complex, to be built in 1993/4, may include a tramway as a link to car parks and the local rail station.

BELFAST

Proposals put forward by Northern Ireland Railways for creation of a light rail line by conversion of the Bangor suburban railway, street operation in the city centre, and a new alignment to Andersonstown were included within a wider study on the future of the city centre carried out by the Northern Ireland Department of the Environment with the help of consultants. The study is still in progress.

BIRKENHEAD

An 800 m standard gauge heritage tramway is under construction to link Woodside Ferry Terminal with the Transport Museum as the first stage of a link to the docklands redevelopment area, and two double-deck replica cars built by Hongkong Tramways have been delivered to permit operation to commence in late Spring 1993. These trams arrived in Blackpool for commissioning trials on 1st October 1992. The line is being authorised under a light railway order. The total cost of the project is around £2 million.

BIRMINGHAM

See West Midlands.

BLACKPOOL

Efforts to identify options for a good-value LRV from eastern Europe have been frustrated by the conflict in Yugoslavia (with the Duro Dakovic factory in Slavonski Brod now on the front line), and management changes at CKD Tatra as the Czech government tries to find a western partner to inject capital in to that company. The municipally-owned Blackpool Transport Services Ltd may be transferred to the private sector in 1993, while the Borough Council is faced with the £5 million cost of renewing the seafront electrical supply system which serves the tramway, Illuminations and street lighting. A short diesel tramway on the refurbished North Pier was opened in September 1991.

BRIGHTON

A brief for a more detailed study of public transport options (including light rail and trolleybus) identified in a prefeasibility study is awaiting a decision by East Sussex County Council and/or Brighton and Hove Borough Councils on whether to proceed. Brighton Borough Council has produced a seafront strategy that includes a heritage tramway to link the western promenade with Volks Railway.

CAMBRIDGE

After identification of a 15 km north-south light rail line, linking park-and-ride transport interchanges with the city centre, work is proceeding on the development of proposals for congestion-pricing of road users to restrain car use and raise the necessary funding for the £70 million scheme. Public consultation expected in 1992 was delayed to permit evaluation of cheaper guided bus options, and a choice between kerb-guided buses and GLT is now being made.

CARDIFF

Detailed studies of public transport needs in the Cardiff Bay area have been carried out jointly by the Development Corporation, City Council and South Glamorgan County Council. These included investigation of light rail, and alternatives such as GLT guided bus technology. The results never emerged for public consultation, but are believed to have favoured GLT, even though this is an unproven product. However British Rail has made clear its preference for better integration of local rail lines with the city centre and Bay development by through-running LRT on the Karlsruhe principle, and further studies are in progress. See also the article in this issue of Light Rail Review.

CHEDDAR

A local consultant has proposed a £10 million tramway to provide a 5 km link between the Cheddar Gorge tourist attraction and a large new car park, thus relieving serious traffic congestion on the highway.

CHESTER

The Cheshire County Council proposal for light rail in this historic city progressed through a detailed feasibility study which confirmed the viability of the £45 million project, and attracted an offer of private funding from civil engineering contractor A F Budge. It was hoped to submit a Bill to Parliament in November 1991, with the support of Chester City Council. However the City decided to postpone any decision on the scheme until the review of the County structure plan and City local plan is completed in 1993, so the project is dormant at present.

CLEVELAND

Consultation on the light rail proposals for the Middlesbrough and Stockton area prepared by consultants showed public support for the scheme, with a preference for street operation linked to the Middlesbrough – Saltburn railway alignment (although it is not yet clear whether the necessary co-operation from BR will be forthcoming). Financial advisors to the County Council have told local businesses that the scheme is a viable investment. The County Council's first priority is for a 13.5 km line linking Stockton with Teesdale, Teesside Park, Middlesborough, North Ormesby and Ormesby, estimated to cost £68 million. However local bus operators have claimed that guided bus could achieve better results at less cost, and further studies have shown that conventional bus improvements are the best medium-term option with light rail alignments protected for the longer term.

DARTFORD

The Borough Council and Blue Circle Industries are still evaluating a fixed-track public transport link between the town centre and the proposed Blue Water Park development alongside the river Thames.

EDINBURGH

Plans for a two-line light rail system were further evaluated under the Joint Authorities Transportation and Environmental Study carried out by Lothian Regional Council and the Scottish Office. This endorsed the light rail proposals and recommended road pricing as an option. Public consultation on light rail resulted in proposals for the city centre tunnel to be extended to 4.4 km, increasing the cost of line 1 to £300 million at 1991 prices. The region's Transportation Committee decided that further work on the Metro should be suspended pending a decision on the package of long-term measures recommended in the JATES report. In the meantime a busway study has been commissioned for the alignment of the proposed east – west line 2.

GLASGOW

Public consultation on public transport initiatives, which included light rail on new alignments, converted BR lines and on street in the city centre, took place in 1991/2. With a positive response to light rail in areas not served by the existing BR network, the Regional Council decided in October 1992 to proceed with a 40 km light rail scheme in north Glasgow, but drop plans to convert south suburban BR lines to LRT. The north Glasgow proposals would see the city centre linked with Drumchapel, Maryhill, Easterhouse, Balornock and Tollcross. Further appraisal of the £180 million scheme will take place in 1993 to develop route priorities, phasing and detailed engineering plans in readiness for an order-making procedure to be started. The Strathclyde PTE evaluation of a possible peoplemover system to link Paisley (Gilmour St) station with the airport is now the subject of consultation.

GLOUCESTER and CHELTENHAM

A pre-feasibility study for a light rail scheme in the Severn Vale area showed encouraging results, and after consultion with private sector interests on joint funding, Gloucestershire County Council has commissioned a detailed transportation study of public transport options which could be effective in containing traffic growth. This will include examination of LRT.

GUILDFORD

Nothing further has been heard of the private company established to promote a £30 million fixed-track transit system linking the University, industrial estate, hospital and BR station with the town centre.

HASTINGS

The Borough Council is considering a heritage tramway for the seafront.

LANCASTER

The City and County Councils considered a proposal for light rail between Lancaster, Morecamble and Heysham, using existing or disused rail alignments, and concluded that LRT could be a long-term option, although bus priority measures were needed boost public transport use in the short term.

LEEDS

After previous disagreements, the West Yorkshire PTE, Leeds City Council and Leeds Development Corporation produced a joint transport strategy including light rail and guided bus schemes. Light rail proposals for four lines were identified, with the first between Middleton in the southern suburbs, and the city centre, via Belle Isle and Hunslet, estimated to cost £58 million. In the city centre tracks would be on street as part of proposals for a pedestrianisation and traffic management scheme, using Boar Lane, Park Row and Cookridge Street to a terminus by St. Anne's cathedral. After public consultation, a Bill for line 1 was submitted to Parliament in November 1991. The Bill also include powers for a guided bus demonstration project in the A61 and A64 corridors. Progress has been delayed by negotiations with the Department of Transport on the proposal for the light rail line to cross slip roads to/from the M1 motorway under traffic light control. Public exhibitions have been held on two further routes to Headingley and East Leeds (Seacroft and Whinmoor).

LEICESTER

A consultants study for a north—south light rail line showed that the scheme could cover its operating costs and produce significant non-user benefits. However Leicestershire County Council decided that there was no realistic chance of securing Section 56 funding in the forseeable future, and the scheme

is not being pursued, despite support within the City Council, which is seeking protection of the alignments.

LIVERPOOL

The Merseyside Development Corporation and the PTE have not announced whether preliminary investigation of light rail opportunites will be pursued.

LONDON

Docklands Light Railway.

The major institutional change has been the transfer of ownership of the railway from London Transport to the London Docklands Development Corporation. This was announced by the Prime Minister in his Guildhall speech in November 1991, and implemented from 1st April 1992. The new management decided to introduce a prime contractor to take responsibility for the efficient execution of all new and upgrading works, and this task was awarded to Brown & Root/Booz Allen & Hamilton on a three-month trial basis from October 1992, with success to be rewarded by a two-year contract. Double-track operation of the Bank extension started on 29th November 1991. Following the closure of West India Quay station for demolition on 11th October 1991, transfer between the city and Stratford branches was switched to the new three-track Canary Wharf station. The Stratford service uses the central reversing track here. The original 11 German-built P86 cars have been sold for around £3.6 million to the German city of Essen, which is converting them to pantograph current collection and manual driving for use on its expanding Stadtbahn system. Four cars had been delivered to Essen by November 1992, with the remainder to follow in 1993. The 10 BREL-built P89 (12−21) cars had their doors rebuilt from folding to sliding operation during 1992. Stations south of Canary Wharf have now been extended to take four-car trains, concluding with one platform of the Island Gardens terminus on 8th June. This date saw the introduction of a revised timetable and service pattern with eight-minute headways:
- Bank−Crossharbour (Island Gardens at peak periods).
- Tower Gateway−Island Gardens (Crossharbour at peak periods).
- Stratford−Canary Wharf.

Major civil engineering work on the £210 million Beckton extension was completed in summer 1992, but minor finishing work at stations and the new depot (where P92 cars 45−91 are stored) was still in progress in October, when delivery of BN-built stock was eight short of completion. First operational trials on the Beckton line were made with P90 car 35, retrofitted for SELTRAC operation. When commissioning work is completed in the first quarter of 1993, consideration will be given to the introduction of a SELTRAC-system shuttle service between Poplar and Beckton, prior to implementing plans for a full integrated service later in the year. Evening shutdown at 21.30, and no weekend service, is expected to continue until July 1993. DLR carried 7.9 million passengers in 1991−92. As the Bill for the Lewisham extension makes

▶ The original delta junction at West India Quay on the DLR has become a segregated flying junction in readiness for the inauguration of City to Beckton service. The BN set has just left Poplar for Canary Wharf, while in the distance a SELTRAC-equipped car is running on the future Beckton line.   *M.R. Taplin*

▶ By October 1992 DLR car 10 had been moved to the new Beckton depot to become the fourth LHB car to return to Germany for the Essen system.
M.R. Taplin, courtesy John Mowlem plc

◀ The interior of the new Beckton depot with finishing work in progress.
M.R. Taplin, courtesy John Mowlem plc

progress through Parliament, four consortia have been shortlisted for the £150 million design, build and operate contract, which it is hoped can be tendered as soon as Royal Assent is received.

Croydon.

A Bill to secure approval for the £140 million Tramlink scheme is being promoted jointly by the London Borough of Croydon and London Transport: submitted in November 1991, it was being considered by the Lords Committee in November 1992 and is hoped to complete all its stages before the Summer 1993 parliamentary recess. In the meantime work has continued behind the scenes to put together a private sector consortium to underwrite the detailed design and specification before final decisions on funding can be made. On 23th October 1992 the promoters signed a project development agreement with an international consortium made up of the British civil engineering contractor Tarmac Construction Ltd, the German vehicle and electrical contractor AEG Transportation Systems, and the French transport operator Transdev, which will provide in excess of £1 million in private investment to take the scheme to contract tendering. The agreement provides that if the consortium is not the successful tenderer for the contract to build and operate the system, then the successful tenderer will have to refund its development costs. Subject to Parliamentary progress and funding, construction work could start in 1994 for initial public service in 1996/7.

Kingston.

A feasibilty study for a light rail network based on Kingston-upon-Thames was funded by the London Borough, London Transport and Surrey County Council, and recommended a 13-km line from Kingston to New Malden, Chessington and Epsom, estimated to cost £80 million. Work is continuing on a second-phase study.

Harlesden – Hanger Lane

The London Borough of Brent has secured City Challenge funding for a study of a high-quality public transport link to serve the Central Middlesex Hospital, which is remote from existing rail lines. Light rail is one of the options to be examined.

Wood Green – Alexandra Palace.

There has been no progress on the London Borough of Haringey's plans for a tourist tramway link to Alexandra Palace due to lack of funding for the feasibility study. Interest has been expressed in the Parry ultra light rail system as an interim measure.

Barking.

The London Borough of Barking Unitary Development Plan calls for light rail links from Barking to Beckton (connecting with the DLR), Ilford, and new development along the Thames at Barking Reach. A 1.5 km heritage tramway may be built to link the town centre and railway station with a planned Tesco superstore.

General.

Friends of the Earth have proposed a north – west London equivalent of the Croydon scheme by using light rail to link Mill Hill, Edgware, Stanmore, Harrow, Sudbury, Wembley and Ealing in a 21 km scheme estimated to cost £120 million. Ernst & Young, the administrators of Canary Wharf, are suggesting a private-sector funded tram network for London to ease pressure on the underground and bus systems. London Transport are taking the first steps to look at light rail potential between central and south London.

LUTON

A working group including BR, Bedfordshire County Council, Luton Borough Council and London Luton Airport is examining the potential for a 2 km peoplemover link between the airport and a new BR interchange station on the Thameslink service.

MAIDSTONE and MEDWAY TOWNS

A consultants study into rapid transit potential showed that the case was not strong, but should not be ruled out as a long-term option.

MANCHESTER

Now that the Manchester Metrolink system is in full operation and making an operating profit, consideration is being given to further extensions. Manchester is making a bid to stage the Olympic games in the year 2000, and is making plans for an extension of Metrolink to the proposed Olympic complex at Eastlands and beyond to Tameside. Other extensions planned are to Salford Quays, Oldham, Rochdale and Manchester Airport.

MILTON KEYNES

Plans to carry out a light rail feasibility study have been postponed due to lack of funding.

NOTTINGHAM

The Bill for the 14 km £68 million light rail line from Nottingham station to Babington and Hucknall was submitted to Parliament in November and under consideration in Committee from June 1992. The promoters of the Bill, Nottinghamshire County Council, Nottingham City Council and Nottingham Development Enterprise have secured £500 000 in private-sector contributions towards the promotion costs, by issuing non-interest bearing loan notes which can later be converted into equity in the joint venture company Greater Nottingham Rapid Transit Ltd. A detailed study is being carried out in to the option of joint running with British Rail on common tracks between Wilkinson Street and Hucknall.

OXFORD

Consultants have carried out a general evaluation of options for easing congestion by improving public transport, including heavy rail, light rail and busways, and consultation on the suggestions is now taking place.

PETERBOROUGH

The City Council is trying to raise funding for a feasibility study of a light rail network.

PLYMOUTH

A pre-feasibility study identified potential for LRT in the Devonport−City−Plympton corridor, and this will be considered further in an area transportation study now being carried out by the County Council.

PORTSMOUTH−FAREHAM

The study to examine the eligibility of the £86 million, 14 km Portsmouth−Gosport−Fareham light rail scheme for Section 56 funding included comparison with guided bus options, and showed light rail would produce an operating surplus, as well as generating maximum decongestion benefits by attracting more private motorists. A good case for Government

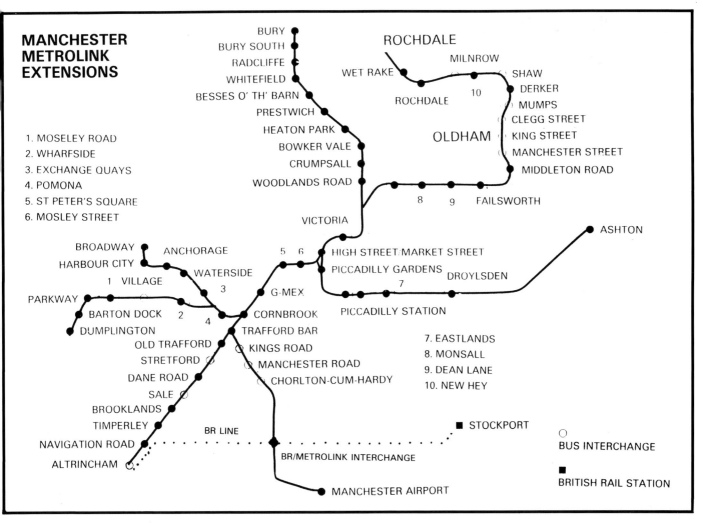

MANCHESTER METROLINK EXTENSIONS

1. MOSELEY ROAD
2. WHARFSIDE
3. EXCHANGE QUAYS
4. POMONA
5. ST PETER'S SQUARE
6. MOSLEY STREET
7. EASTLANDS
8. MONSALL
9. DEAN LANE
10. NEW HEY

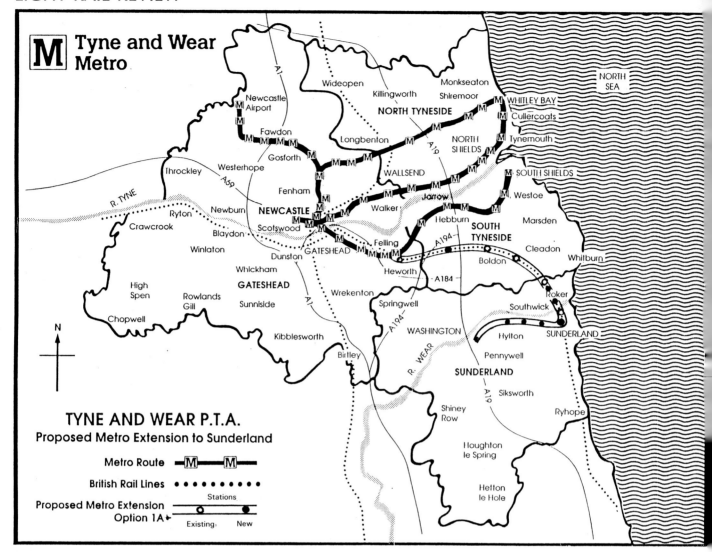

Ⓜ Tyne and Wear Metro

TYNE AND WEAR P.T.A.
Proposed Metro Extension to Sunderland

Metro Route ⬛Ⓜ▬▬Ⓜ⬛
British Rail Lines • • • • • • •
Proposed Metro Extension ──○────●──
Option 1A ←   Stations
           Existing   New

grant was proved. The County Council is now carrying out a public consultation exercise to obtain views about the proposed route and possible options, before a final choice is made, environmental impact study commissioned, and order-making procedures commenced. People's Provincial Buses, Gosport Ferry Ltd and Badgerline Rapid Transit have set up a joint operation SeHants Overground to promote the GLT system for this link.

PRESTON

Lancashire County Council has completed an internal study of options for a park-and-ride link from the M6 to Preston, including light rail on former railway alignment. Public consultation is expected in 1993.

SOUTHAMPTON

A major transportation study has been commissioned by Hampshire County Council and Southampton City Council to develop options for public transport investment. A parallel technical research study with Nottinghamshire County Council will examine the scope and feasibility of joint operation of light rail and BR trains on the same tracks on the Karlsruhe principle.

SOUTH YORKSHIRE

Whilst construction work is under way on phase 1 between Sheffield City Centre and Meadowhall, the rest of the system to Mosborough/Herdings and Middlewood/Malin Bridge is at various stages of construction or detailed planning. Meanwhile, park-and-ride sites are under consideration, as are possible extensions to the system. These could involve new routes to Rotherham, possibly via Orgreave and Treeton, with a possible cross-Rotherham route starting with a major park-and-ride site near the M1 north. In addition, consideration is being given to the possiblity of converting a stretch of the ex Great Central main line to light rail.

STOKE-ON-TRENT

Results of a public transport study for North Staffordshire are due to be published shortly. Options evaluated included bus, rail and light rail.

SWANSEA

West Glamorgan County Council has commissioned consultants to develop a 10-year transportation strategy, including investigation of light rail opportunities.

TYNE & WEAR

Public service on the 3.5 km Metro extension from Kenton Bank Foot to Newcastle Airport (£12.25 million, with a £2.36 million contribution from the airport company, and £2.45 million from the EEC) started on 17th November 1991. A phase 1 report on the Washington and Sunderland extension study was produced in summer 1991, identifying alignments and financing opportunities. Options included three corridors (Pelaw–Sunderland, Washington–Sunderland and the recently-closed BR Leamside line) with an exclusive metro line, or in the case of Pelaw-Sunderland possible joint running with BR trains under a form of automatic train protection. After consultation further studies have been carried out and the preferred has recently been announced. This is the Pelaw–Sunderland option, extended along the south side of the Wear using the closed BR Penshaw route to a park-and-ride site at South Hylton adjacent to the A19. The service can be worked using existing rolling stock resources. A five-year programme to refurbish the 90 metrocars is in progress, with car 4087 acting as the prototype for a new livery and revised interior seating. Some single-track sections of the South Shields line are being doubled to increase capacity. The system carried 500 million passengers in its first 10 years of operation, and is currently handling some 43 million passengers/annum.

▶ Hong Kong built Birkenhead tram 69 comes out of the container ship Peninsulor Bay at Southampton Docks on 10th September 1992.　　　*C.N. Smith*

WARRINGTON

The Borough Council and Cheshire County Council have a working party considering public transport options, including the potential for light rail.

WEST MIDLANDS

The government commitment to fund line 1 of the Midland Metro (Birmingham–Wolverhampton) once the scheme had met the criteria for Section 56 grant was given in December 1990, but reneged on in June 1992 (see article elsewhere in this issue). Centro is carrying out certain preliminary works, and has now restarted the tendering process to obtain a firm price. It has decided to put funds from the sale of its bus company into the re-opening of the rail line from Snow Hill to Smethwick, which includes 5.3 km of shared alignment with metro line 1. The Bills for lines 2 (Five Ways–Airport) and 3 (Wolverhampton–Walsall–Dudley) (60 km) have been passed by Parliament, with the exception of a short section of street running on line 2 in Chelmsley Wood, which is now the subject of a late amendment of alignment to meet objections upheld by the Lords. This will see the Airport line using Chester Road on the edge of the estate, while a short spur along Moorend Ave will give a branch terminus at the shopping centre. Consideration is also being given to changes to

line 2 that would be necessary for it to serve InterCity's proposed Birmingham Heartlands station. Bills are in Parliament for an extension of line 1 in tunnel from Snow Hill under the city centre to the Bull Ring development, for a spur from line 2 to serve the Castle Vale estate, and for an extension of line 3 from Dudley to Brierley Hill to reach the Merry Hill shopping centre interchange. The light rail proposals for Coventry have been shelved after studies showed they were unlikely to meet Section 56 criteria for 15 years.

WEYMOUTH

The Borough Council has commissioned consultants to evaluate the possibility of using disused BR tracks between the station and the quay to provide a tramway service.

OTHER SYSTEMS

The 1.7 km monorail line serving the Merry Hill retail centre at Dudley in the West Midlands closed on 20th June 1992 for "six weeks"of essential maintenance. However public service had not been resumed by December.

The ultra light rail demonstration line built by Parry Peoplemovers at Himley Park model village near Dudley commenced public service in mid-September. 72-volt battery power is used to charge a flywheel on a small 14-seat railcar, which can then run for about 4 km before recharging is required. The company is promoting the system for peoplemover-type shuttles and operation in city centre precincts, and demonstrations using portable track have been carried out in a number of locations.

◀ The flywheel-powered ultra light railcar at Himley Park, with the 72-volt battery-powered charging rail in the foreground.　　　*M.R. Taplin*

▲ As well as delivery of eight new trams for regular service (641–8 of 1984–88), Blackpool has had one-man car 7 rebodied as a replica vintage tram by Bolton Trams Ltd. This modern version of the traditional open-sided crossbench car has been used on Promenade summer specials since 1988.
J.F. Bromley

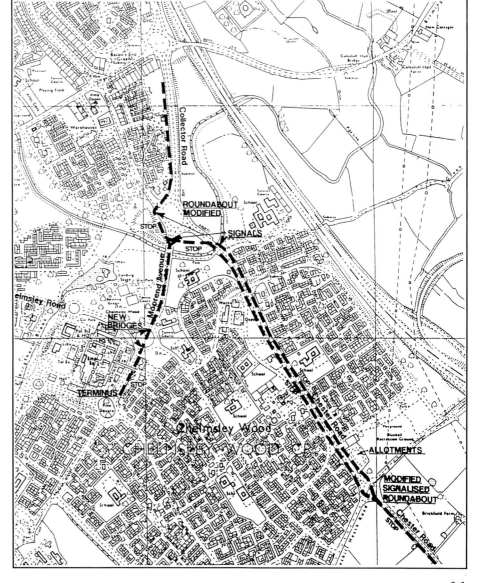

▶ The amended route of Midland Metro line 2 in Chelmsley Wood.

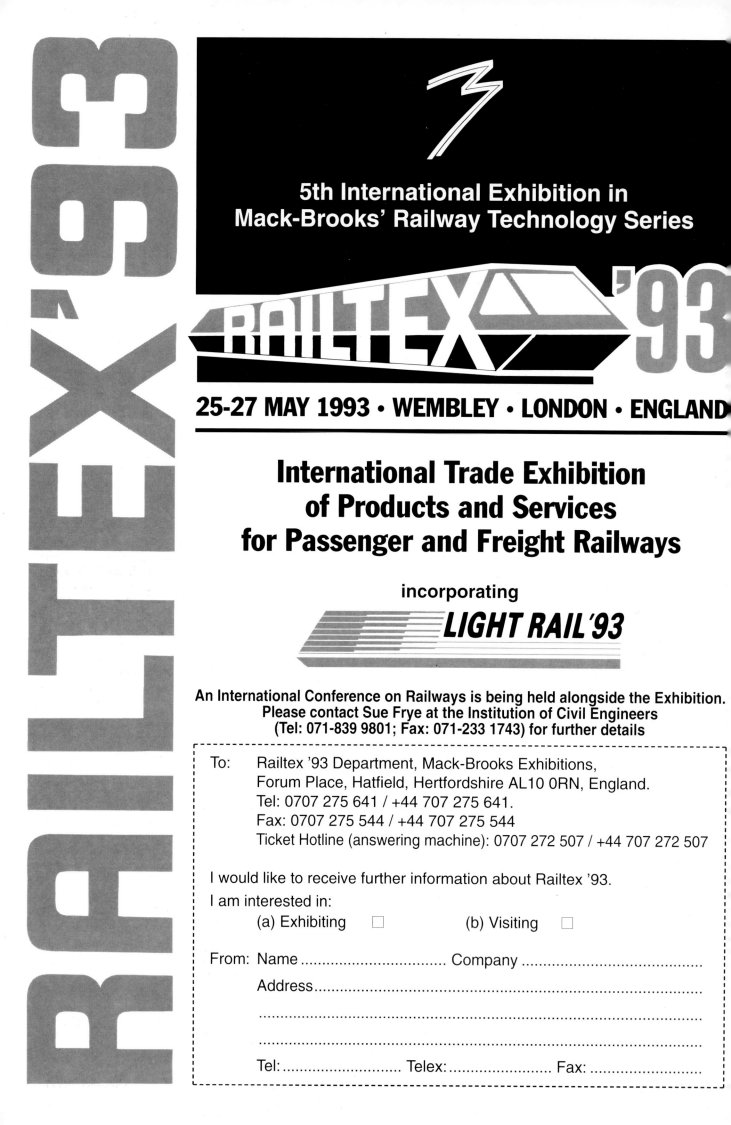

5th International Exhibition in Mack-Brooks' Railway Technology Series

RAILTEX '93

25-27 MAY 1993 • WEMBLEY • LONDON • ENGLAND

International Trade Exhibition of Products and Services for Passenger and Freight Railways

incorporating

LIGHT RAIL '93

An International Conference on Railways is being held alongside the Exhibition. Please contact Sue Frye at the Institution of Civil Engineers (Tel: 071-839 9801; Fax: 071-233 1743) for further details

To: Railtex '93 Department, Mack-Brooks Exhibitions,
      Forum Place, Hatfield, Hertfordshire AL10 0RN, England.
      Tel: 0707 275 641 / +44 707 275 641.
      Fax: 0707 275 544 / +44 707 275 544
      Ticket Hotline (answering machine): 0707 272 507 / +44 707 272 507

I would like to receive further information about Railtex '93.

I am interested in:
      (a) Exhibiting ☐   (b) Visiting ☐

From: Name .... Company ....

Address..

....

....

Tel: .... Telex: .... Fax: ....

FULLY-ACCESSIBLE LIGHT RAIL
The West Coast USA Experience
by Andrew Braddock, London Transport

This paper describes a visit he made to the USA and Canada in 1992.

During an all too brief holiday last April, I had the opportunity to see all the US West Coast light rail systems, the trolleybus tunnel in Seattle and Vancouver's "Sky Train", too. A tight schedule covering eight cities in nine days meant that only a cursory glance at each of San Fransisco, San Jose, Sacramento, Los Angeles, San Diego and Portland was possible, but in each case we were lucky enough to meet people from the operating company to talk about their system and plans for further development.

More than a little drama was added to the trip by the after-shock of an earthquake felt on our first night in California and by driving into Los Angeles on the night the Rodney King trial verdict led to rioting. Added to this was a "mild" 103 degree heatwave the day of the visit to Sacramento!

By way of background, I should mention that there is federal legislation in the United States requiring public transport operators to make their services accessible to people with disabilities, including wheelchair-users. In many cases this is achieved by the provision of "paratransit" (like Dial-a-Ride in London and other UK cities) but there is widespread use of lift-equipped buses in regular service in the majority of US urban areas — including all the West Coast cities with light rail.

Interestingly, Seattle has about the most extensive provision of lift-equipped buses (including all the original trolleybus fleet and the new dual-mode vehicles operating the tunnel services) and this leads to what seems, at least to European eyes, to be a much higher number of wheelchair-users out and about in the city. The combination of a highly accessible transit system and widespread provision of what the Americans call "curb cuts" (dropped kerbs to us!) clearly offers a "network" of routes for wheelchair-users to follow — even in a hilly city — and the result is that they do!

SAN FRANCISCO

Our rapid transit tour began with the San Fransisco Municipal Railway, whose "Muni Metro" light rail network is being developed to provide better access in accordance with the 1990 Americans With Disabilities Act. The downtown two-level subway, with the BART heavy rail line below the Muni tracks, is essentially fully accessible. At each of the stations there is at least one lift from the street to the ticket hall and on to the two platform levels, with straight platforms and only a small gap both horizontally and vertically between platform edge and the floor of the Boeing-Vertol cars. Unassisted access is possible for wheelchair-users. In the subway section, the Muni Metro cars run with the steps at all doors (other than the front entrance next to the driver's cab) raised to the level of the high platforms in the stations. Away from the tunnels, the system operates in the street or along at-grade reservations so the steps are lowered to suit boarding from low platforms of about pavement height or from the roadway.

In order to provide full access outside the subway, Muni is gradually introducing the concept of "handicapped platforms" at key stops on the light rail lines to the west and south of the city centre. This involves the construction of a short section of raised platform with ramped access from the street, against which the driver places one of the LRV doors by pulling up at a "Handicapped" marker in the track bed. Apart from the cost — so far only eight stops have this feature - the real difficulty presented by this solution is that wheelchair-users are made to feel different with the use of the term "handicapped platform" and the fact that the car stops in a different place to pick them up. There is a time penalty, too, since the steps at the relevant door have to be raised and lowered again before the car can depart. That said, it is difficult to see what other choices Muni might have made but they will be closely examining the option of low-floor cars to replace the elderly and unreliable Boeing fleet in the next few years.

SAN JOSE

After an interesting trip against the peak flow on the commuter rail link from San Fransisco funded by CalTrans (the California State Department of Transportation) our next port of call was San Jose. Very much part of Silicon Valley this modern city has seen enormous growth in industry and housing over the last ten years, and its Guadaloupe Corridor light rail line was planned with yet more growth in mind. Another example of low platform/high car-floor design, the Santa Clara County Transportation District's line is obviously much newer than the streetcar-based San Fransisco network. It therefore benefits from a planned approach to access for disabled passengers and a radically different solution to the problem of getting wheelchair-users on board the Canadian UTDC-designed LRVs has been adopted.

At all stations there is a large stainless steel box on a concrete plinth at the leading end of the platform for each direction of travel, which contains a lift and a bridge-plate for use when anyone in a wheelchair wishes to board or alight. The car pulls up with its front door (nearside or offside depending on whether there is a side or island platform) right alongside the lift box. The driver then steps out of the car to unlock the roller shutters either side of the box and operates the mechanism. The lift platform folds out and lowers to ground level to the rear of the box — away from the platform edge - and when it is raised to car floor level the bridge-plate drops down to eliminate the gap between lift and car floor, above the steps in the doorway. Thus a smooth transfer of a wheelchair-user from about pavement level to the floor of the car is achieved but, as can be imagined, the process it both cumbersome and time-consuming!

With the benefit of a fully-accessible design from the start, San Jose does have the edge over San Fransisco in offering the opportunity for wheelchair-users to travel to and from all stops, and this is reflected in much higher use of the system by that group of disabled people. But the approach is still essentially "separatist" in that only one door of the car is available for access (as the driver needs to step out to the platform to open the lift box, etc.) and, perhaps more importantly, wheelchair-users have to wait at the lift box away from other passengers. Like San Fransisco, the LRV effectively stops in a different place (or in once case was seen to make two stops) if a wheelchair-user is waiting to be picked-up.

SACRAMENTO

On, then, to Sacramento the Californian State Capital — and another fine example of a new LRT system. Here, the Siemens-Duewag U2 design cars give one the impression of Frankfurt in the sun and service appears to operate with Germanic reliability. Again, the combination of low platform or street level loading and high-floor cars presented a challenge for Sacramento RTD, and a solution broadly similar to that adopted at the surface stations of San Fransisco's Muni has been selected to ensure full access to this city's "Metro". In most cases, this involves provision of a long sloping ramp up to a short raised section of platform at the outer end of each stop. At some central area stops there is insufficient space for a straight ramp so a rather steeper spiral approach is used. At the suburban ends of the initial LRT line there is single-track operation with stops featuring two raised areas to meet the need for wheelchair-user access at the leading car door, next to the driver, for both inbound and outbound trains.

Once more, a waiting wheelchair-user dictates a different stopping point and, in common with the two systems described so far, requires fairly accurate "spotting" of the car by the driver as the width of each raised platform is only slightly greater than the door width. The procedure for boarding and alighting is, however, much simpler than either San Fransisco or San Jose. The raising of the doorway steps of the former, and the use of wayside lifts like the latter, is replaced in Sacramento by a simple drop-down bridge plate, operated by the driver, which covers the horizontal gap between raised platform and the car floor — over the U2's standard three-step doorway.

Whilst essentially the simplest of the options seen throughout the visit, the Sacramento system does still require a separate waiting point for wheelchair-users, and often leaves them exposed to the elements on a raised section of the platform whilst their able-bodied counterparts have a shelter in which to wait. Admittedly, rain seems to be much less of a problem here than in, say, Manchester! — but the "separatist" tone is still present.

LOS ANGELES

After returning to San Fransisco to sample a few more of the delights of this fascinating city (not least of which is the much cooler climate) we then headed south to Los Angeles.

Our plans included hiring a car to drive down the California coast on the historic Highway 1, and on the approach to LA came news over the radio of the rioting breaking out in the South Central area of the city. Mention by the "on the spot" reporter of the name of the street in which our hotel was situated did little to ease the tension, but study of the street plan for this vast metropolis quickly demonstrated that "Figueroa" stretches some 23 miles from south to north and we were going to be well away from the trouble. At least, that was the situation at about 19.30! As the night wore on, and the inevitable American approach to TV news-reporting across nine channels gave a blow-by-blow account of unfolding events, our hotel ended up being much closer to the rioting than at the start. With the mounting tension in the city the next day, we took advice from Southern California Rapid Transit District and abandoned our official visit to their downtown headquarters and headed instead for Long Beach and the hopefully more peaceful end of the Blue Line — SCRTD's first new-generation light rail installation. Though it seemed much further away from the troubles than it actually was, the strikingly modern city of Long Beach had all the atmosphere of somewhere expecting the same ugly scenes

as South Central LA at any moment. Wise counsel suggested a brief "walkabout" would be appropriate, before making for an earlier train from LA to San Diego than was originally planned!

The Blue Line is unquestionably an impressive beginning to a series of much-needed public transport investments in the Los Angeles region. The very fact that the world's principal motor car city is having to invest millions of dollars in something which was close to extinction in the 1960's is fascinating. Light Rail in Los Angeles is the subject of just as much political controversy as it is in the UK, but the big difference is that in Southern California the debate is not about whether to fund it at all but about how much more of the money raised already can be spent quickly to attack the legendary "gridlock" congestion throughout Los Angeles! From the accessibility standpoint, SCRTD have capitalised on the benefit of a high platform/high car floor system. The sophisticated Blue Line LRVs are equipped with a ride-height levelling mechanism which ensures virtually level access between platform and car and, because there is no need to get people in wheelchairs up from ground or low-platform level, the Los Angeles to Long Beach line is the only one of the US West Coast systems to provide genuinely integrated facilities for the group of users, at all doors on all journeys.

Interestingly, the local Long Beach Transit System operates a number of Canadian-built "Orion" low-floor minibuses which also cater for wheelchair-users and connect with the Blue Line at the city's downtown "Transit Mall". From the limited view we had of the system, the surface stations appear to follow a standard pattern of access by ramp at one end of the platform and by steps at the other. The only problem wheelchair-users appear to face is getting across the street to the LRT reservation in California's constant flow of traffic.

SAN DIEGO

The role model for much of the United States resurgence of interest in the tram was the next stop on our rapid tour. San Diego's "Trolley" was without doubt, the most impressive light rail installation I have seen outside Europe. The decision to adopt a virtually standard German LRV must have been taken with immense difficulty, given the strength of "Buy American" politics, but it has paid of handsomely. Of course, Duewag cars are now assembled in California so the elected representatives can genuinely point to a high US-content in the more recent deliveries to the Metropolitan Transit Development Board. The approach of MTDB has been well-documented elsewhere, so suffice it to say here that their policies in San Diego have produced a first class co-ordinated public transport network. The rapidly-expanding LRT system is the key feature of this network, and its provision for wheelchair-users represents yet another solution to the problem. The bulk of the U2-design vehicles have a lift fitted at the front door on one side of the car only so that, in the usual configuration of a two-car train, "back-to-back" coupling ensures the provision of a lift for either direction of travel. This alternative arrangement for a low-platform/high car floor system actually provides the swiftest access we saw for wheelchair-users, but is achieved at the expense of sterilising one doorway as the lift is a permanent fixture. The lifts themselves are extremely reliable (unlike many of those fitted to buses) and fairly simple to operate. The driver can actually stay in the cab to operate the controls, and delay to the service is minimal even when — as we saw on two occasions — there are two wheelchair-users waiting to board. Perhaps the only small criticism is the appearance on the platforms of the international wheelchair symbol to indicate where people in wheelchairs should wait and, as is the case with the raised platform section in Sacramento and the liftbox in San Jose, the driver only pulls up alongside the symbol when there is a wheelchair-user waiting. In the case of San Diego

San Francisco's Muni Metro has key stops equipped with ramped platforms for wheelchair access.   *M.V. Ballinger*

The marker between the tracks on the Muni Metro light rail system tells the driver where to pull up at accessible surface stops.   *A.J. Braddock*

t is not clear why a *separate* stopping point is required, though it is necessary on the other two systems as the front door could be used by other passengers boarding from the rest of the platform.

Having paid a visit to Mexico, across the border from San Diego Trolley's South Line terminus at San Ysidro, we then flew up to Vancouver, BC for a rapid tour of "Skytrain" and the accessible bus network of that beautiful Canadian city. Skytrain offers excellent access, though it is not strictly a light rail system, with near-level boarding from platform to car and some excellent signing to the lifts which are a necessity at all of its stations.

PORTLAND

On, then, to Portland and "MAX" (Metropolitan Area Express) as this city's LRT line is called. Again, the combination of high-floor cars (from BN/Bombardier) and low platforms requires a mechanical means of boarding for wheelchair-users, and here there are wayside lifts similar in concept to San Jose but of completely different design. The lift is enclosed in a box at leading ends of platforms but the "box" is open so that a wheelchair-user actually waits inside it for the driver to step out of the car and get him aboard. There is perhaps less to go wrong with this arrangement but the passenger waits with rather less dignity and, of course away from all the able-bodied users. On raising the lift platform a bridge plate automatically extends to eliminate the gap over the steps in the car doorway, and the wheelchair-user is able to board or alight.

The design criteria for Portland's west-side light rail line, which will connect in the city centre with the existing Banfield Corridor line, were being completed at the time of our visit and an excellent report had been produced on the findings of a study of European LRT systems undertaken by the Project Team. They looked in detail at the low-floor cars coming into service in Germany and Switzerland, and recommended that the new line in Portland should have 100% low-floor vehicles. Options such as the insertion of a low-floor centre section into the existing six-axle high-floor cars, to run alongside the desired new fleet, were being examined too, and it looks as though Tri-Met will be the first US authority to invest in a low-floor fleet.

SEATTLE

The next visit was our last, before the long flight home. As already mentioned, Seattle ranks highly as an "accessible city" and warrants a mention in Light Rail Review because the new trolleybus tunnel is equipped with tracks ready to take LRVs as and when the system is upgraded. No less than

245 Italian-built articulated dual-mode buses have been delivered to Seattle Metro, and they operate as diesel vehicles from a wide range of points in the northern and southern suburbs to and through the city centre. At the stations at either end of the tunnel, the vehicles turn into trolleybuses with a sophisticated raising/lowering device for the trolleybooms. The stations are all built to an extremely high standard of design and finish, and each one is well-equipped with lifts to all platforms in addition to escalators. The buses themselves are fitted with front door automatic lifts which convert the step at the entrance into a flat platform that rises, under the control of the driver, to the high floor level of the vehicle. At the time this large fleet was ordered, the development of low-floor buses had not reached North America so it is perhaps unfortunate that what is otherwise an excellent example of a rapid transit line − which can progressively develop from bus to light rail − which is fine for wheelchair-users − the three steps at each door do present problems for the majority of disabled people (who are not in wheelchairs), for elderly passengers and for those encumbered with heavy baggage or travelling with young children (with or without a baby buggy!)

CONCLUSIONS

The experience of seeing the approach to public transport access in the eight cities visited was most useful. There is no doubt that great efforts have been made to meet the needs of disabled users − especially those in wheelchairs. My only criticism is that, because the "rights issue" has focused particular attention on that group − the minority of disabled people − less has been done to meet the needs of visually impaired and ambulant disabled passengers.

Clearly, the trend towards low floor buses and trams in Europe has now taken hold. In London we shall be experimenting next year with the first low-floor buses built to right-hand drive configuration, and hopefully the Croydon "Tramlink" scheme will soon bring low-floor LRVs to the capital too. The benefits of the low-floor concept are that it meets the needs of *all* public transport users and, by removing the steps, not only is simple and quick access made available but services are actually speeded up for everyone as boarding/alighting time at stops is reduced. Low-floor light rail vehicles can also eliminate the "separatist" approach I have referred to since all doors should be useable by all groups of people. "Access for all" is now a realistic objective for urban transport, and the work done in North America has undoubtedly given much food for thought.

Andrew Braddock is the head of the unit for disabled passengers, London Transport

◀ A Muni Metro Boeing car at one of the accessible platforms. The gap between the platform and the car floor could present a problem for the small front wheels on many manual wheelchairs.   *A.J. Braddock*

▼ Once opened up, the simple van-style lift can be lowered to pavement level to collect a wheelchair-bound passenger, and then raised to floor height for access to the car.*A.J. Braddock*

▲ Santa Clara County Transit UTDC-built car 842 pulls up alongside the lift box fitted at all light rail stops in San Jose.   *A.J. Braddock*

▼ A bridge plate is lowered from the car to provide level access for the waiting wheelchair user to board.   *A.J. Braddock*

▲ The lift mechanism on a San Diego car prevents normal access through one door. *A.J. Braddock*

The San Diego lifts are simple, reliable and relatively speedy to operate. *A.J. Braddock*

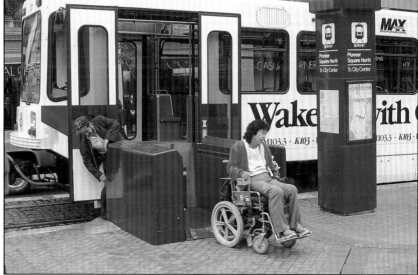

▲ The wayside lift used in Portland is located at the leading end of each station; wheelchair users are told to wait inside the box. *A.J. Braddock*

▶▲ The driver must descend from the car the unlock, activate and lock-up the Portland lift. *M.V. Ballinger*

▶ The ex-Melbourne trams on Seattle's heritage line have had their drop centres built up to permit wheelchair access. *A.J. Braddock*

◀ Los Angeles has managed to get a minimum horizontal gap and no vertical step between platform and car floor. *A.J. Braddock*

CANADA
● Vancouver
● Seattle
Washington
● Portland
Oregon

USA

California

Nevada

● San Francisco
● San Jose

● Los Angeles

San Diego ●

MEXICO

SOUTH YORKSHIRE SUPERTRAM

Construction and Detailed Design in Sheffield

by Peter Fox

The South Yorkshire Supertram project is the largest public transport infrastructure project in the United Kingdom outside London since the building of the Tyne & Wear Metro. A major feature on the project was carried in Light Rail Review 2, together with a progress report in Light Rail Review 3. Now that construction and detailed design work are well underway, it is pertinent at this stage to review the progress being made, and to explain how the concept is being turned into reality.

DESIGN AS YOU GO

At first sight, the title of this feature seems rather strange, as design work would be expected to precede construction. However, in the Sheffield scheme, the two processes are being carried out at the same time, so that whilst the first phase of the project (previously referred to as 'line 2' because it was the second line to get parliamentary approval) is being constructed, other phases are still in the detailed design stage, and in some cases have not yet reached that stage. This causes misunderstandings with concerned members of the public, who are completely mistified when they are told in all honesty that SYSL don't yet know the exact alignment of certain sections of route! This method is being used in order to speed up the implementation of the scheme. Whilst it would be preferable to design the whole scheme in advance and then construct it, this was not possible since no funds were available for this purpose in advance of the funding of the whole scheme.

CONSTRUCTION PROGRESS

At the time of writing, construction of Phase 1 of the project, from Sheffield city centre to Meadowhall is at an advanced stage. The first signs of progress appeared with the start of construction work on the many bridges which are a feature of this phase. It is useful at this stage to list these for the benefit of the reader, in order of location starting in the city centre.

- Commercial Street bridge (bowstring arch design).
- South Street bridge (from Park Square to Interchange). Of post-tensioned segmental concrete construction).
- Parkway Viaduct (also post-tensioned segmental concrete).
- The bridge over the BR Midland Main Line near to Bernard Road (Steel girders).
- Parkway bridge (the bridge over the Sheffield Parkway road between Aston Street and the depot).
- Woodbourn Road bridge (a concrete bridge over the Great Central main line).
- The Canal bridge (steel arch).
- Darnall Road bridge (concrete).
- The River Don bridge at Tinsley (steel girders).

One aspect of the construction process which required careful phasing was the yonstruction of the many street crossings on this phase. Phase 1 is, of course a light railway rather than a tramway and features no street running. Construction of the street crossings required many traffic diversions and in many cases streets on which crossings were required were used for diversions whilst the crossings were being constructed on other streets.

All track on phase 1 is BS11 - 80A 80 lb/yd flat-bottomed rail, supplied by British Steel Track Products of Workington, laid on sleepers consisting of concrete blocks with steel ties. The street crossings are also laid in railway rail with a steel section alongside to provide an edge for the concrete, except for the one on Woodbourn Road which has been laid using grooved tramway rails.

The brickwork for most of the station platforms on phase 1 has been laid, but as yet none of the surfaces or furniture have been fitted. Incidentally, SYSL is using the term 'tramstop' rather than 'station'. The terminology in this case is a matter of personal preference, but the author prefers 'station', believing a tramstop to be just a pole with a sign on it, possibly with an adjacent shelter, whereas what are being constructed in Sheffield are low platforms, hopefully with a high standard of fitting out. Presumably the term 'tramstop' is being used so as not to imply a structure which the public might interpret as causing major disruption on the street sections of future phases.

Poles for the overhead supply have been erected over most of the route. The same three types of pole as were used in Manchester are being used, but most of them are of the narrowest type, the diameter of which is virtually the same as that used on the poles in Sheffield's former tramway system which was abandoned in 1960.

Most of the poles now have the support arms fitted, but main line wiring was not commenced until 23rd February 1993 from the Meadowhall station end.

Work is also underway on Phase 2 which takes the line from behind Sheffield Midland station through the Norfolk Park Estate. The concrete supports for the Norfolk Park Viaduct are now in position, and work has started on the downhill trackbed on Park Grange Road, the major road through the estate. Service diversions are also being undertaken on other Phases.

PUBLIC CONSULTATION

The detailed design work which is proceeding on the future phases is being accompanied by what must be one of the most challenging public relations exercises ever attempted in the UK. The introduction of a light rail system into the fabric of an old established urban setting, which includes many areas of residential property is one which has not been attempted this side of the English Channel in recent times. Understandably many citizens of Sheffield are fearful of the unknown and have attempted to scupper the plans over many years. This is despite the fact that Sheffield was the last city in England to operate a tramway.

Manchester and Tyne & Wear obviously had consultations with interested parties, particularly city centre traders etc, but as those systems operate predominately on ex-railway alignments consultaion with suburban residents was not required. The Sheffield scheme is in many ways the reverse of those two, with a major part of the project on highway

▶ A view of the Parkway Viaduct under construction. The triangular junction will be on the traffic island to the left (see page 2). In the left background, just above the second lighting standard from the left is the Royal Victoria Holiday Inn, the venue of the Light Rail Transit Association's 1993 annual general meeting.

▼ The Viaduct is of post-tensioned segmental concrete construction, as shown in in the views below of the underside of the viaduct and of one of the sections waiting to be hoisted in position.

Peter Fox (3)

◀ The bridge over the BR Midland main line is of steel girder construction and its positioning necessitated possession of the main line. The operation was carried out on 20th November starting at midnight. Here one of the two steel bridge decks is seen being hoisted in position at 01.00 on a bitterly cold night.

Peter Fox

▲ The elegant bridge over the Sheffield Canal between Woodbourn Stadium and Technology Park. The bridge is of steel arch construction with longitudinal girders on top and a concrete deck.

▶ The double-length platforms are under construction at this station which will serve both the Sheffield Arena (shown in the background) and the Don Valley Stadium. In front of the stadium is the East End Park on which a ladle previously used for casting molten steel has been erected as a symbol of the Brown Bayley steelworks which used to be on the site. To the right of the two LRT tracks are the BR single line and the Sheffield Canal.

▼ The terminus at Meadowhall Interchange with overhead wires in position on 23rd February 1993. The platform is under construction. *Peter Fox (3)*

alignment, running past housing, both council and privately owned. This without doubt brings the present activity into the area of pathfinding. Hopefully Sheffield's near neighbour – Leeds, and Croydon will look carefully at the exercise when they set about consultations.

The way the consultation has been operated has brought three distinct elements to play:
1. Consultation with property owners fronting the tramway alignment.
2. Formal consultation by way of exhibitions and meetings.
3. On street and newspaper information regarding traffic disruptions etc.

With the exception of mentioning that all owners of property in the city centre fronting the tramway have been contacted concerning the use of building fixtures in place of poles, which has brought a very positive response, this article will only cover section 2, as section 1 deals primarily with confidential items between the parties concerned, and section 3 is an area which is constantly changing to suit circumstances.

EXHIBITIONS AND PUBLIC MEETINGS

As the draft alignment for each phase of the scheme is finalised, Sheffield City Council initially consider the proposals before the details are put forward for public consideration. Usually exhibitions are arranged in a suitable venue followed by a publicised meeting. So far phases 1 (Meadowhall to City Centre and Interchange), 2 (Interchange to Hillcrest), 4 (West Street to Netherthorpe Road), 5 (Hillcrest to Gleadless Townend) and 6 (Gleadless Townend to Donetsk Way) have been dealt with. The response varies from place to place, with interesting differences of opinion being recorded. Some areas are telling the authorities that more stations are required, whilst in another area a petition has been started recently to prevent any stops being built at all!

The consultation has resulted in certain changes having been made to the plans. Two cases illustrate this point. On City Road, residents and traders complained that there would not be enough parking spaces, and the plans have been modified with the addition of two large parking areas. On Ridgeway Road (the outer ring road between Manor Top and Gleadless Town End), the original plans for a 'trambaan' have been altered because the necessary road widening would have resulted in the felling of a large number of trees. It has therefore been decided to run the LRT tracks as a tramway down the outer lanes of the dual carriageway. To do this all the way along Ridgeway Road could result in unacceptable delays at Manor Top in the 'to City' direction, and therefore a segregated alignment is provided at the side of the road for a short distance on the way to Manor Top.

Not all suggestions have been accepted, however. Indeed, many of them would have proved impossible to adopt. In particular, it has not proved possible to put in all the extra stations demanded, as this would have resulted in unacceptably prolonged end-to-end journey times. One interesting point to note is that because of Sheffield's hilly terrain, most bus passengers tend to get off buses at the stop above where they want to be, but get on at the point below where they want to be. This will obviously continue to be the case with Supertram. At the bottom of the steeply graded Park Grange Road, by the Norfolk Park Viaduct, however, there is no planned station and the local residents, many of whom are elderly would have a very steep climb to the station at Park Grange. This is one situation where the residents' request for a station should, in my opinion, have been heeded. A straight section of track is being provided at this point, so that there is the possibility of a station there in the future. This particular case has resulted in the alienation of the residents, who have to put up with a viaduct opposite their bedroom windows, but get no benefit from the scheme.

Regrettably there has been a dearth of information supplied by the specialists, particularly in handy leaflet form, and this has given the opponents of Supertram a chance of circulating adverse comments about future fares, environmental problems dangers of crossing roads with trams operating etc. A great number of people have not been told about the great benefits of Supertram or at least have not bothered to find out about it, and it is now very common for the public to utter negative comments, which leaves public education as a major factor in the coming months.

It is of course very easy to be critical with hindsight, but this author believes that more contact with Sheffield's citizens will bring immense benefits to the scheme, and should be looked at urgently.

IMPLEMENTATION OF THE PROJECT

The project is being implemented by a project team which was appointed by South Yorkshire Passenger Transport Executive (the PTE) to manage the implementation of the physical works forming the project. The project team subsequently become responsible to South Yorkshire Supertram Ltd. (SYSL) as client when this (presently wholly-owned) subsidiary of the PTE was formed. The team comprises Turner & Townsend Project Management (TTPM) with Kennedy & Donkin Transportation (KDT – formerly Kennedy-Henderson) and Turner & Townsend Chartered Quantity Surveyors.

The project team's primary task is to ensure that the infrastructure and trams are handed over to SYSL and its operators and maintainers on the due dates, within the identified project budget and duly functionally tested, so that SYSL can proceed with training and trial operation. It is appropriate to note here that the well-publicised eight phases are identified purely for construction management purposes. Public opening stages and dates have not yet been defined.

The actual major decisions on final alignment are taken by a committee which has representatives of the PTE, the city council, SYSL, TTPM, KDT and DBS*.

As part of the Project Team, KDT have been and continue to be responsible for a number of distinct areas of work.
● Technical support to the Parliamentary work for the 2nd, 3rd and 4th bills, all now being acts.
● Preparation of Tender documentation including specifications for the two main contracts, the management of the tendering process and recommendation for letting of the contracts.
● Design approval, that is technical approval on behalf of the client of all design proposals from the two main contracts. Approval is against the technical specification and in consultation with the client on matters of detail not covered in the specifications which are of a "performance" nature only and do not specify detailed designs.
● Liaison with sub-consultants in the design approval process, principally DBS (Bridges) and DBS (Highways and Traffic).
● Limited quality auditing of the main contractors against their quality plans.
● Inspection of production at manufacturers' works. The majority of this work is for the trams themselves where a resident inspector is employed (provided by Guthrie & Craig of Newcastle upon Tyne) to check all aspects of production. Most infrastructure work on the civil and building parts of the project, is being supervised by DBS resident engineers.
● Site installation inspection of the M&E works for the project.
● Attendance at testing at manufacturers' works to act as a witness for the client of satisfactory performance under

* DBS refers to Design and Building Services, a wholly-owned subsidiary of Sheffield City Council.

test. This may be extented to a similar role during testing on site.

One example of the type of work being carried out by KDT is discussion with HM Railway Inspectorate with regard to clearances for different types of street running. A set of standards has to be agreed for the different types of right of way used on scheme. These then become the standards to which the contractor has to operate. Another area with which KDT have had involvement has been that of signalling design principles for a system designed primarily as 'drive on sight'. A system has to be developed for the integration of interlocked points and their signalling indications on certain sections, e.g. the single line sections.

As Project Manager TTPM contol the three fundamental project parameters of time, cost and quality.
● The establishment and control of the master programme for the project.
● The establishment and control of the project budget and cash flow.
● The management of site supervision staff whose prime objective is to maintain finished quality

TTPM's crucial role is that of managing the project where it interfaces with significant external bodies who exercise or attempt to exercise influence of constraint over the development of the project. The bodies in question are:
● The Planning Authority.
● The Highway Authority.
● HM Railway Inspectorate.
● The Statutory Utilities.
● The Frontagers (the owners or tenants of property fronting onto the LRT system).
● The Promoter.
● British Rail.

The influences exerted by these organisations are legitimate, but the extent to which they could, if uncontrolled, jeopardise planned progress or delivered cost is such that much team effort is expected in managing relationships with the parties concerned.

THE CITY CENTRE

One major feature of the scheme not yet decided upon is the exact route and design of the section through the City Centre. Central to a decision in this phase is Castle Square, a subway complex known to everyone as "the hole in the road". A final decision on what to do with this is expected in the next couple of weeks, but it is likely that it will be filled in, so that the Supertram route will be able to run in a straight line along High Street, rather than have to skirt round the roundabout above.

Another concern is the Cathedral conservation area. This could easily become another 'pole park' like Piccadilly Gardens in Manchester if thought was not given to an acceptable design. The City Council have enlisted the help of Lord St. John of Fawsley's Royal Fine Arts Commission and other interested bodies to ensure that the layout enhances rather than detracts from its surroundings.

By the time 'Light Rail Review 5' appears in November 1993, trams should once again be running in Sheffield, although not in public service. Exciting times lie ahead.

▲ At Alsing Road Crossing, site of the former BR Tinsley West Junction, the line becomes single before splitting into two tracks again at Meadowhall Interchange. The crossing appears unduly acute for what is, after all, the main line of the system and will result in trams having to slow down unnecessarily.   *Peter Fox*

▶ Woodbourn Road street crossing under construction with the grooved tramway rails waiting to be placed in the troughs in the concrete. Coloured patterned concrete has been used for the pedestrian footpath.   *Peter Fox*

▲ and ◀ The bodyshell of the first of
the three-section trams under construc
tion at the Duewag Works in Düsseldorf
R.N.H. Jones, courtesy SYSt

ACKNOWLEDGEMENTS

The author acknowledges the assistance
of South Yorkshire PTE, South Yorkshire
Supertram Ltd., Kennedy & Donkin
Transportation Ltd., Turner & Townsend
Project Management Ltd., Balfour Beatty
Construction plc and Mr. Paul Jackson
for help in the preparation of this feature.

▼ The concrete supports for the Park
Grange Viaduct on Phase 2 of the project. The main BR Sheffield – London line
runs in a cutting in front of this viaduct.
Peter Fox

ROMANIA

Seven New Tramways in Seven Years!

by Michael Taplin

Romania was the first of the communist regimes to collapse, and few will forget the scenes on Christmas 1989 television as the dictator Ceausescu fell from power. This unsavoury despot, called by his acolytes ''the great conductor'' sold most of Romania's oil abroad to raise foreign currency, leaving little for home industry and transport. Thus an agressive electrification policy was pursued throughout the 1980s, with six new trolleybus systems and seven new tramways inaugurated in 1983–91.

At the start of the 1980s Romania had tramways in Arad, Braila, Bucuresti, Galati, Iasi, Oradea, Sibiu and Timisoara, all built before the First World War. Old rolling stock was being replaced by home-built trams of two types, an articulated car assembled in the Bucuresti tramway workshops after the design of the Linke-Hofmann-Busch prototype imported in 1969 (411 were built for Bucuresti in 1973–88) and a bogie car built in motor and trailer form by Banat in Timisoara in 1972–90 (530 examples). Originally equipped with German Kiepe electrical equipment, shortage of currency soon forced substitution of a Romanian copy that became renowned for its unreliability. 371 Tatra trams were also imported for Arad, Braila, Bucuresti, Galati and Iasi — their reliability suffered when there was no money for spare parts.

The electrification programme saw new standard-gauge tramways built in seven cities:

1984 – Constanta (population 325 000);
1987 – Brasov (340 000); Cluj–Napoca (300 000);
 – Craiova (260 000) and Ploiesti (230 000);
1988 – Resita (100 000)
1991 – Botosani (50 000).

172 articulated trams were built in this period, and 127

▲ The Romanian capital Bucuresti, has a large fleet of eight-axle articulated trams built in their own workshops after a prototype was acquired from LHB in Germany. The current desperate financial circumstances mean that maintenance and repairs are kept to a minimum.

► In order to serve routes with stub termini, a double-ended six-axle car was developed.   *M. Moerland (2)*

of the Banat cars. The single tram route in the small town of Botosani was started during the Ceausescu era, but work came to a stop in 1990, delaying the opening by a year. The ruthless urbanisation policy of the old regime involved bulldozing historic towns and cities to build standard blocks of flats and not suprisingly the people of Botosani took some convincing that work underway on this basis to clear a path for the tramway should be finished off.

Today public transport is needed in Romania as never before (the average wage is £31/month, a second-hand car costs at least £1100), but the situation on all the transport undertakings is dire. There is no money for new roling stock and precious little for maintenance. Morale is low. Fares subsidy will disappear from 1st January 1993 because of all level of government are broke. Even the new tramways present a sorry picture, as the photo feature shows. Help from the west for the transport undertakings has so far seen cast-off buses from Bruxelles, Paris and Geneva on Romanian streets. What the tramway undertakings would really like is cast of Tatra trams from the former East Germany, and the spare parts to keep them running.

▲ Severe shortage of capital funds has forced one Romanian city, Iasi, to continue using two-axle cars in service on one of its routes. Several dilapidated unrebodied (or rebodied in the 1960s?) sets such as 79 + 79 — shown at Canta terminus on 26th May, alongside Tatra T3 No. 250 — were still in service in May alongside a few recently-rebodied two-axle-car sets.

◀ Brasov 20, an eight-axle V3A tram, rounds the turn from Strada 13 Decembrie into Bulevardul Garii, on 25th May 1992, westbound on the sole route of this 1987-opened system. The livery of yellow-gold and cream has been simplified somewhat from the original scheme.

▶ The tram system of Iasi is probably the first anywhere in more than 20 years to rebody two-axle trams, in this case using parts from withdrawn four-axle Timis cars. At least two sets wear the new, modern blue-and-white livery displayed here by 100 + 101, which are pictured at the Canta terminus of route 2 on 26th May 1992.

◀ Shortage of rolling stock means that Romanian trams are crowded most of the time, but this is evident in the extreme at factory shift-change times. Iasi, 327 + 327, a packed pair of Timis bogie cars, are westbound on route 5 at Baza III, on 26th May 1992.

▶ The rural tramway between Sibiu and Rasinari renewed its fleet with Timis four-axle cars in the late 1980s. Motor 7 + trailer 6* have just arrived at Rasinari terminus on 25th May 1992 and are about to back into a 'y' (reverser) in a side street. Note the horse-drawn (but rubber-tyred) wagon on the right.
S.J. Morgan (5)

* There definitely exists also a Timis motor 6 and probably a trailer 7 — undoubtedly originally coupled in sets as 6 + 6 and 7 + 7 — so one cannot just write 'Sibiu 7 + 7'.

▶ The most recent of seven new tramway systems built in Romania in the last 10 years was that at Botosani, whose completion was delayed by the revolution. In the meantime the new cars stood in the open and are already badly affected by rust.

▼ Romania is a country of contrasts, evidenced in this view of a modern articulated tram in Braila alongside an earlier but still common mode of transport. *M. Moerland (2)*

▲ In 1968 the port city of Braila built a cross-country tramway to a remote industrial plant. A Timis tram + trailer set is seen on the line today.

◀ A colourful tram set on the new system at Cluj-Napoca passes Empire architecture that still fills most Romanian city centres. The personal embellishments in the cab indicate that drivers tend to work the same shift with the same tram each day.   *M. Moerland (2)*

The Romanian oil fields
re centred on the city of
loeisti, where the tram-
ay undertaking has ac-
uired a new name and
very since the revolution;
now uses the same in-
ials as the Paris transport
ndertaking, RATP.
M. Moerland

◀ Sibiu's solitary tram
routE links the city with its
rural hinterland, running
on roadside track to the
village of Rasinari. New rolling stock has arrived in the
shape of a handful Of Timis
trams, including motor car
6.   *M. Moerland*

▼ Motor car 7 with trailer
6 arrives at the city boun-
dary from Rasinari.
S.J. Morgan

Miscellany

The first of 100 Duewag/Siemens low floor trams for Frankfurt am Main was presented on 17th February. This new design is a three-section double-ended car on three bogies featuring hub drive with three-phase a.c. motors and a 350 mm floor height throughout.

G.H. Köhler

BRITISH-BUILT TRAMS FOR STRASBOURG

The former BR workshops at Derby, Crewe and York, formerly known as BREL Ltd. after privatisation are now owned by ABB. Following problems with the collapse of SOCIMI in Italy, the trams for the new Strasbourg light rail system, are to be built in the UK. The bodies will be built at York and the bogies at Derby Locomotive Works. Final assembly will be either at York or at Derby Carriage Works. An artist's impression of one of the trams is shown here.

The trams are of an innovative design with a low-floor throughout. The bogies are carried under small 'pods' which link the three body sections or carry the driver's cabs. The water-cooled asynchronous traction motors are carried on the otside of the bogies and drive through double-reduction gears to the independantly motorised wheels.

There will be a feature on this vehicle in 'LRR5', together with details of other new low-floor trams. *ABB/Socimi*

AN APOLOGY

Platform 5 Publishing Ltd. would like to apologise for the severe delay in the publication of 'Light Rail Review 4'. A number of reasons conspired to cause the problem, the main ones being the move to new premises, a burglary and the over-running of a large project which should have been finished before 'Light Rail Review' was started. Nevertheless, we hope that readers are happy with it, now that it has, at last, been published. 'Light Rail Review 5' **will** be published at the beginning of November 1993, in time for the Light Rail exhibition being held in Birmingham.

Among features in 'LRR5' will be Leeds, the new Docklands Light Railway Beckton extension, and the modernisation of the Lille—Roubaix—Tourcoing inter-urban system.

OPINION

We make no apology for carrying an article on guided buses in this publication. There exists a view among certain sections of the British political scene that guided buses might offer the same benefits as LRT at a fraction of the cost. Nothing could be further from the truth. A ride on the 'City Express' guided bus in Essen, Germany did nothing to commend bus travel to me. If anything, I would say that the journey was less pleasant than on a conventional bus, since vibrations seemed to be being picked up from the guide wheels.

A bus is a bus and nothing else and the addition of guide wheels will not produce a system which will convince motorists to leave their cars at home and use public transport.

Rail Transportation including Light Rail can and does make a significant impact on modal split. All of the new European LRT systems have been a success and there can be no substitute for doing the job properly. We must treat as suspicious any scheme which pretends similar benefits for guided buses as for light rail. Such pretensions are not borne out by the facts.

Peter Fox

MANX ELECTRIC

An addition to the books listed in the advertisement opposite is a new publication 'Manx Electric'. *Manx Electric* is written by Mike Goodwyn of the Manx Electric Railway Society and contains a wealth of information on the history and operation of both the Manx Electric Railway and the Snaefell Mountain Railway. *Manx Electric* is probably the best value book ever to have been published by Platform 5, containing over 200 A5 pages, 16 of which are in full colour. Specialist chapters deal with traffic, vehicles, tickets, buildings etc. and the book has been produced to coincide with the centenary of the MER. A book not to be missed by anyone whether or not they have ever visited the Isle of Man. Only £7.95 (plus postage & packing).